The Micro Revolution

Peter Large has been technology correspondent of the *Guardian* since 1977. Born in 1930, he was brought up in Barnstaple, Devon, where, after National Service, he began his career in journalism.

Peter Large joined the *Guardian* in 1961. He caught the computer bug when, as production editor, he was involved with the editorial side of the newspaper's use of computers. He then changed course to write about electronics. His only other obsession is cricket. He is married and lives in Highgate, north London.

D5

The
Micro Revolution

Peter Large

Fontana Paperbacks

First published by Fontana Paperbacks 1980
Copyright © Peter Large 1980

Set in Linotype Times

Made and printed in Great Britain by
William Collins Sons & Co. Ltd, Glasgow

Contents

Acknowledgements

My thanks to Peter Preston, editor of the *Guardian*, for giving me the chance to learn about the fascinating world of computers and for allowing me to draw extensively from my newspaper work for this book; and to the many friends I have made in computing's global village for generously giving their time to educate an ignorant journalist.

1. The case for concern

First came the abacus. Twenty-six centuries later man cornered the electron. Today, the computer, powerful but still fairly dumb descendant of those counting beads, is reshaping society. In less than two decades the industrialized world has come to depend on the computer; government, commerce, defence could no longer function without it.

The changes – so far – have been made with unsensational effects on employment and daily life, and the benefits have been immense, in medicine and science as well as in administration. But this quiet revolution has produced a few horrors and many niggling annoyances, caused by inadequately planned computer systems and the scarcity of computer-skilled people. It has also bred a new class of criminal. And it has led to the accumulation of huge data-banks of personal information which, if uncontrolled, could threaten individual liberty.

Now the process is accelerating. The kind of post-industrial society which was forecast by the futurologists when the computer was in its infancy is becoming reality. The microscopic circuitry of the computer chip – built into a razor-thin sliver of silicon which can be less than a quarter of an inch across and cost less than £1 to make – now does work that required a roomful of machinery twenty years ago. Today, £500 buys computing power that cost £10 millions when the computer industry began.

The chip's revolutionary impact stems from its size. It's cheap because it's small; it's fast because it's small (the electronic messages don't have far to travel); and, because it's small, it can be used in places where computers would not fit before. Therefore it brings to reality what used to be simply computer-science theory – the theory that the computer can perform any task which its human instructors can precisely define.

This alters the rules in much the same way that the futurologists of the 1950s forecast; it heralds the shift towards an economy in which the 'knowledge industries' are predominant and manufacture is relegated to an automated sideline. The doctrine is that information is wealth, and wide and swift access to information is power. Therefore, knowledge is becoming the key economic factor, demoting the traditional factors of production – land, labour, raw materials, and capital. Scientific advances in farming have reduced the amount of land required per unit of production; now the silicon chip will automate farming further and also reduce the amount of land required for factories and offices; the need for captial lessens as the chip finds ever-cheaper ways to supply goods and services and as the knowledge basis of the post-industrial society encourages even further the credit-based economy; and the chip brings greater efficiency in the employment of raw materials and reduces the consumption of energy.

All that, so the theory goes, we can expect over the next two decades. Certainly, a slower-moving version of the process was visible before the micro-chip matured; factory employment had already begun to shrink, as did farm work in the first Industrial Revolution.

Now much wider areas of human labour can be taken over by ever-cheaper microelectronics. And the jobs that disappear are not confined to the distasteful and the dangerous. Computer design systems can perform – faster and better – most of the routine work of the draughtsman and the designer; the skills of the printer and the ploughman are being automated too; microcomputers, called word-processors, are replacing the typewriter and the typist; the greater speed, capacity and flexibility that are becoming available in telecommunications and in the storage and manipulation of information are threatening the functions of middle management; computers that contain the distilled knowledge of leading specialists could make humdrum, or destroy, the work of many professionals – lawyers, family doctors, tax consultants.

Nevertheless, the orthodox view is that (other factors being equal) microelectronics will create more employment opportunities, though different ones, as all technological advances have done so far. The reasoning is that the creation of greater wealth, through greater efficiency, will once again expand the demand for services and new products – though, this time, with greater upheavals in employment and with a need for people to retrain for several different occupations in a lifetime.

The heterodox view is that the chip will put many millions out of work in Western Europe and North America before 1990. The doubters argue that for once history *is* bunk: the changes will be so rapid and so widespread as to make past experience a poor guide, and new areas of possible employment will themselves be susceptible to automation. Therefore, they say, we must demolish the Protestant work ethic and displace employment as the crucial arbiter of how wealth is distributed. If we succeed in a massive reorganization of society, then the road to Utopia is said to be open once again – the end of all uncreative work, the emergence of a new, rich, mass leisured class. If we fail: mass riots of the unemployed, followed by the collapse of democracy, followed by (computer-controlled) totalitarianism, whether of left or right.

Those choices may sound science-fictional, but they are being expounded by an increasing number of academics and trade union leaders and by a few politicians who are prepared to think on a ten-year rather than a four-year scale. The argument cuts across political boundaries. In the debate that swept through Western Europe and beyond in the final years of the 1970s, the belief in an orthodox, if hasty, transition to fuller automation has been shared, on the whole, by the political establishments of left, right and centre. In Britain, for instance, in 1979 a Labour Prime Minister was followed by a Conservative one in presenting essentially the same arguments about the opportunities of the chip. Equally, the radical view is heard right across the political spectrum, the voices differing only in the ideological details of how the machine-created wealth would be redistributed among those freed from work.

That inconclusive debate has, however, produced one point of virtual unanimity: in a competitive world there is no alternative to using the chip as quickly and widely as possible, to update products and services and to automate production. If the people of any one nation do wish to cling to jobs that are no longer necessary – and, indeed, may have become literally counter-productive – then they must also be prepared to accept a sharp drop in material living standards.

Whichever route we in Britain choose – or find ourselves forced along – few of the army of pundits would challenge the verdict of the former British Labour Minister, Tony Benn: 'The changes in society will be absolutely phenomenal and could make the 1980s politically very difficult to handle.' It is difficult, in fact, to conceive of a single industry or business which can ignore the micro-chip. The danger is that many of us still refuse to believe it: we could wake up too late. We have all, young or old, lived through a period that has inured us to increasingly rapid change. Those who can remember the world of thirty years ago would then have ridiculed the idea that they would soon watch, from their firesides, men driving a car on the moon. But the chip – which was created partly to serve that very exploration – is bringing encounters of a closer kind. Its eventual impact (and eventual here might mean less than twenty years) could be more fundamental than the nineteenth-century shift from the land to the cities.

The aim of this book, therefore, is to help to close the credibility gap; to illustrate that tomorrow began yesterday and that the options sharpen and tighten every day. It will try to show some of the dangers – and the glittering prizes – that lie ahead. It will not get entangled in technical detail, but it will attempt to explain the processes and the machines that are building a post-industrial world, whose currently fashionable label is the Information Society. The emphasis throughout will be on the factual evidence around us today – not on the guessing games of futurology.

Nevertheless, Chapter 2 does begin the job with a bit of fiction – but it is fiction that owes little to theories or imagination. The future lifestyle it sketches is based on microelectronics in use today or in the research pipeline. It makes a lot of blissful assumptions about man's humanity to man. Later chapters look more sceptically at the problems: not simply the horrendous task of social reorganization (particularly in class-ridden societies like Britain's) but also the technical dangers involved in committing ourselves to a machine we do not always understand. After all, computers are rigidly logical: people are not.

2. A day after tomorrow

Jane Babbage is striding along a Cornish tide line. But for her and her terrier, the wintry beach is deserted. Jane Babbage is also at work: organizing a worldwide newspaper with 1·5 million readers.

Her office is cupped in her hand. It looks like a cross between a pocket calculator and a walkie-talkie. It is a computer, a TV set, a phone, a filing cabinet, a library, a typewriter, a teleprinter, and a secretary. Through that little box, she can talk to a reporter in Seoul; organize the morning video conference of her fellow executives scattered around the UK; or dictate to a computer 4000 miles away a memo that will be delivered to all her American staff within a minute.

Jane is a features editor on a new breed of newspaper: a specialist, twice-daily, world journal. Hers is called *Finance Today*. It has no printing presses and no headquarters – unless you count the computer centre run by a few technicians, where the one master copy of each page is produced.

Finance Today looks much like a 1980 newspaper except, of course, that all the pictures are in colour. It is distributed direct to the home by space satellite and/or fibre-optic cables. (Fibre-optics – the use of light signals travelling along hair-thin glass tubes – began to replace electric cables in the telephone networks in the early 1980s.) The customer orders *Finance Today* by tapping a few keys on his home computer or simply by speaking to the machine. A facsimile copy then flops out of the laser printer attached to the computer. Simultaneously, his bank balance is debited.

Newspapers serve specialized sectors of the global village because of the multitudinous sources of immediate information. True, the UK has only three TV channels devoted solely to news and five to education, but the growth of computerized information services has outpaced expectation. Worldwide networks bring to the home anything from a technical treatise in the library of Calcutta University to the price list of the village supermarket. These networks also enable the customer to cross-question computers in which the best minds in such fields as tax or property law have distilled their knowledge. But Jane and her family still like to read in solid form. Their cottage contains a few expensive paperbacks and a massive microfilm library.

Many of the readers of *Finance Today* buy the whole paper, but on most days there is an article or two that might appeal to a wider audience. These are advertised on the TV news channels and the information networks, and people often buy just one page of an issue.

Jane's beach walk ends with a debate with the paper's design editor (who lives on the Isle of Man) about the layout of the current features pages. While Jane is strolling back to her cottage, the design editor is doodling with a light pencil on his computer screen, trying to find the ideal pattern for his first page. Later, he will adjust on the screen the details of text, headlines, and pictures; and when he is satisfied with the result, he will send his final instructions by landline to the computer centre in what remains of Birmingham. There are no editorial people at the centre, only a few engineers and a couple of computer programmers.

The security of Jane's decision-making walk relies on an elaborate sequence of codes. Her UHF (ultra high frequency) radio link is to her home computer and to the computer that runs the local ComCent (communications centre out of Newspeak and phone exchange in old English). ComCent is no longer prepared to rely on the automatic call sign to establish identity. Both Jane's own computer and the district one analyse her voice with greater than human certainty and will respond only to that voice linked to that call sign. The central computers of *Finance Today* also require her signature, written on her own screen.

Back home, Jane can now spare an hour for her new book on the international monetary system. She is in the middle of a chapter on the consequences of the British decision to close the Mint, within five years, now that virtually all transactions are cashless.

Jane is a traditionalist. She likes to see the words as she writes. Therefore the desktop computer in her study has an antique keyboard with letters. As she types, the words appear on the screen before her. The computer corrects her spelling and, on its irritating days, argues with her about grammar and punctuation. Few people are still prepared to bother with the discipline of the keyboard; they dictate their letters and instructions to the machine and let it get on with them.

The computer stores Jane's book on floppy discs, like flimsy, miniature gramophone records. (Here, too, Jane is old-fashioned: she likes this archaic and bulky method of storing information because she understands vaguely how it works.) She can recall the chapters to the screen for revision and the computer will then shape the words to fit the particular page format of her book. The small printer attached to the computer will reproduce each page in its final glossy form, ready for satellite transmission to her New York publisher. Thus the publisher has no printing to organize, only distribution via the networks. Within a few hours of her keying 'End' the book can be on sale anywhere.

Jane's work is interrupted by the arrival of her husband, Joe. He has brought home the village plutocrat, Nathaniel, to mend the guttering. Nat is seventy-three. He was a farm-worker in the days before automation. Now he does most of the jobs in the village that cannot yet be robotized economically, like collecting the refuse for sorting at the district recycling plant. He used to have a brisk line in window cleaning, but home robots are encroaching on that. Jane and Joe (a GP) are poor. Their jobs are interesting, there is keen competition to train for them, and they therefore receive little more than the basic national wage that everyone gets for doing nothing. But the village is prepared to pay big money to Nat.

Nat has become an entrepreneur. His most profitable venture so far has been to turn his smallholding into a cornflakes farm. Nat's computer-driven electric van takes itself off on a regular pre-programmed weekly run around the West Country, delivering orders of the famous (and costly) Nathaniel brand of non-synthetic cornflakes, complete with bogusly rustic picture of Nat on the packets. Nothing in this enterprise involves Nat in manual work. His factory-farm is run by one capsule. That capsule first uses microwaves to wriggle rather than plough the land. Then it hovers over the ground to release, at the required intervals, seeds, fertilizers, pesticides and so on. Chemical sensors monitor growth, and the capsule's time-release mechanism adjusts to changes in the weather. In between times the capsule becomes the first intelligent scarecrow. Finally, machines, also run by microelectronics, handle the harvesting, processing and packaging of the crop (the packaging material is grown on a field rented from a neighbouring farmer).

Nat's arrival prompts Jane to turn to home chores. She turns on the house robot and tells it 47 ('follow me'). She leads it to the door of the dining-room and says 39. That is the new program for cleaning that room now that the table has been moved nearer the window. The robot sets off to vacuum the carpet and dust the chairs and table. It will return to the door when the job is done. In fact, Jane nearly stumbles over the little, spider-armed box in the doorway five minutes later, and has one of her rare pangs of materialistic envy. She cannot afford one of the newer models which deal in words not numbers, which can hold in their memories a week's household routine, and which go to a power socket to recharge themselves when their power runs down.

At least the twins, aged eight, seem to have exhausted their propaganda campaign for a teaching robot more chatty than their tiny model. But that thought only recalls to Jane's mind the sole area of marital dispute: education.

Jane's and Joe's job categories mean that they can get exemption from sending the children to the reopened village school: it is assumed they will ensure that the twins follow the appropriate syllabuses of the national school TV network, which includes an interactive (talking back) element. Jane hankers for the old, direct encouragement of the personal teacher of her school and university days. Joe accepts the orthodox theory that is now applied in almost all professions: it is better to use the skills of the most gifted individuals for the benefit of all – whether the required advice is medical, legal, horticultural, or whatever.

A mellow ping sounds through the cottage, a ping that punctuates Joe's side of the argument. It is a call for his services. He turns on the living-room wall screen as he answers the computer. The call comes from the manager of riding stables, thirty miles away on Bodmin Moor. His house is an old two-storey place and he has fallen downstairs. He thinks he has broken his ankle. He holds the ankle up to the miniature TV camera which is linked to his personal computer, and the ankle appears grotesquely magnified, in livid colour, on Joe's wall screen.

After the usual does-it-hurt-there? and wiggle-your-toes routine, Joe is seventy per cent certain the ankle is not broken. But to be sure that he has covered all the necessary ground, Joe calls the medical information bank. He cross-questions a computer which has refined and arranged the information poured into it by a leading orthopaedic specialist (a Mexican, as it happens). That prompts him to bring the possibility of spinal injury from the back of his mind to the fore.

He therefore upgrades the urgency of the X-ray he was about to order, and calls up the patient's medical records via the UPI. The UPI – Universal Personal Identifier – was introduced into Britain after an anguished debate about personal privacy, although it had been in use in many countries since the 1970s. Each citizen has a code number assigned to him and that number is the key through which a complete personal dossier can be built by correlating the wide variety of personal information held in many different but interlocking databanks.

Use of the UPI is restricted by other code numbers and, in certain cases, signature checks. Thus Joe can read on his computer screen the medical records of anyone in Britain, provided that person is ready to disclose his number. But Joe's code authority will not allow him to use the UPI to take a look at a patient's police record, bank balance or rent arrears. Most people carry their number with them so that if they are involved in an accident, the medical help they receive will be based on the fullest information. The cautious also carry a radio bleeper to summon help if they are away from the beaten track.

Joe is about to leave, rather late, for his round of visits when a neighbour calls to complain of a niggling stomach ache. Joe slots in the appropriate program cassette and leaves the computer to question his neighbour. 'Please, mark the spot where the pain is with an X on the drawing that will now appear on your screen' ... 'Is the pain there all the time?' ... There might be forty questions and Joe will have a printout of all the information contained in the answers awaiting his return.

Meanwhile, Jane is in the kitchen preparing dinner. She selects a recipe from the computer memory, then sets the cooker to have the soup ready at 18.45, the main course at 19.00, and the sweet at 19.25. Then it's back to work.

The key daily conference of *Finance Today* begins at 16.30 Greenwich. Then the final shape of the evening (UK) edition is decided and the possibilities for the breakfast issue are discussed. Jane calls in the twins from the garden; they like to sit and watch, though the entertainment – Jane's face popping on to the screen five times larger than life – is intermittent. The first face on the wall screen is that of the chairman and editor-in-chief. He is one of the thirty per cent or so who still prefer urban life. His house-cum-office is in the newish North Bank development of London. The capital still exists, though no longer as Dylan Thomas's 'eight million headed village'. Suburbia has melted. The streets are silent and fumeless. Traffic is sparse.

The City itself also still exists – spread around the country. It is third to the communications and entertainment industries as an export earner. (Britain finally lost out in manufacturing in the early 1990s, failing to match the price and quality of the totally automated factories of the rest of Western Europe, North America, and the Far East.)

The conference produces several feature ideas that will need to be tackled quickly. As soon as it ends, Jane's voice is bouncing from the satellite to correspondents here and there. She does not have to tap out or even look up their long 'phone' numbers. She tells her computer 'Desai, Karachi' and the computer finds the number in its memory and organizes the connection. She can do the same with her pocket computer. In fact, on summer days she likes to do all her work on the beach. She then carries a second pocket computer which can be plugged into the communications one. That second box is packed with permanent memory chips. It holds hundreds of phone numbers and will also store scores of newspaper articles.

Actually, Jane could carry all that information around in her wristwatch but, again because of her sensible lack of interest in the details of the technology that underpins her workstyle, she has not updated her equipment. It takes several indignant memos from *Finance Today's* technical manager, complaining about her 'non-compatible antiques', before she will try something new.

Jane's spell of duty ends at 18.30. She works twelve-hour shifts with six other joint feature editors. The editor who takes over has caught up with the plans at the conference. Also, of course, he can call to his screen for editing or re-editing all the material being poured directly into the computers by his scattered reporters.

Jane now turns her attention to the personal electronic mail that has piled up in the day. The computer screens a few notes from friends, a reminder of a local theatre company rehearsal, and two voting requirements, one local, one national. Normally, Jane's attention would go to the local issue, since national administration has shrunk to a framework. But today's national question concerns her directly. Should membership of NIB be cut from twenty to ten and should its elections be held annually instead of biannually?

NIB – the National Informatics Board – was formed in 1988. Just as the British government awoke belatedly to the importance of microelectronics in the 1970s, so it was too late in appreciating the concomitant importance of telecommunications in the changed economy. NIB took over from the Post Office, leaving it to the dying functions that its name covered. Then, as the TV channels grew, NIB took over the supervisory role there as well, checking monopoly tendencies in the media.

Jane had been invited to take part in the TV debates on NIB's wider role – the debates that had replaced Parliament in a direct democracy – and her decision is quickly taken. But the code precautions before she presses the computer key to record her vote are the most elaborate in her code-ridden life. She makes a mental note to check the national decision on the 22.00 news.

The local issues are more complex. Should the district solar power fields be extended to reduce family reliance on their own roofs and windmills when the national grid cuts down to factory and communications power only? Should the district buy more street-cleaning robots to serve the villages as well as the town? Vote Two is easy and a bit malicious – one more Nat enterprise down the drain. Vote One is shaming. Jane has not made time to look at this question properly and, since voting is compulsory, she enters an abstention. Energy has become an even more ticklish problem since the international convention putting restrictions on the applications of nuclear power.

That done, Jane prepares for the awkward evening ahead. Her brother is due on the 19.30 hovertrain for a weekend visit, and those rare weekends tend to descend into a tri-angular argument. John is a systems consultant – he has just finished supervising the trials of the unmanned coal-mines under the North Sea – and his wandering life makes Jane feel that she and her family are anti-social in having lived in one area for nearly three years. Equally, John's delight in gadgetry for gadgetry's sake irritates Joe.

But a more serious argument could develop this time. The national decision had been taken, only a month before, to make the payment of the basic wage automatic: till then it had been paid to the self-employed and the non-workers only after they had completed a minimum of ten hours' public work in any week. John's message, accepting the weekend invitation, had included a tirade against the 'laya-bouts' whose vote had won the day. This inevitably annoyed Joe, who had regularly campaigned in the village's nightly TV debates against this forced labour when so little un-skilled work was required.

Jane therefore chooses her one safe, if boring, alternative for the evening. She calls national channel 14 – one of the four central sports channels – and orders a forty-minute video recording summarizing the day's play in the cricket Test match in Sydney. When it is replayed, John will delight in showing his skill at their editing console, pulling a corner of the picture into slow-motion close-up at Joe's direction, or dividing the screened action into four.

The one tinge of embarrassment comes when John asks how his Christmas present (a home coordinator system) is behaving. Jane and Joe never use it. But before waving out the bedroom lights, Jane guiltily sets the controls; the waking buzz at 07.45 will now simultaneously part the bedroom curtains, raise the central heating to sixty-five degrees, disengage the burglar alarm, turn on the breakfast, unlock the front door, and send the robot out to clear the footpath of snow.

3. Do we want to work?

How quickly a Babbage way of life happens – or whether it happens that way at all – I would not dare to forecast. If you want the alternative horror scenario, jump ahead to Chapter 14, which shows that a doubleplusgood Orwellian world could just as easily be produced by the same technology.

But this book is in itself a rough measure of the pace of change, for it has had to be revised several times in the few short months of its preparation. It will almost certainly be out of date once again by the time you read it. Already most of us have elements of Jane Babbage's world in our daily lives. Word-processors, like Jane's, are replacing the office typewriter; desktop computer terminals, linked to national and international networks, are commonplace (you have relied on them for years every time you book a flight); there are authors today working exactly as Jane worked; a few doctors are already using the computer as consultant and interviewer of patients.

The evidence for the more esoteric items is also around us: computers that recognize and obey the individual human voice, computers that talk, computers that read handwriting and detect forgeries, minute memory chips that hold a million pieces of information, electronic transmission of letters and newspapers, instant voting by computer, robots that could replace the coalminer as well as the factory worker ... It's all old-hat.

But Chapter 2 did slightly bend the rules (that nothing should be included that is not already on sale or clearly recognizable in the research laboratories). One bit of marginal cheating was the pocket office: all the pieces exist but, as we shall see later, there is a little more squeezing to be done before it is all in one package. Also, the ultra-high radio frequencies would probably have to be in general use before you could talk to Hong Kong while walking down Fifth Avenue.

Another debatable item is Nat's farm. Within the rules, one could have driverless tractors guiding themselves through the crops by sensors, which respond to lights or radio beams placed to define their path, or by the human ploughman guiding the robot-tractor through its first furrow. Machines that use microelectronics to extend the robot-harvester's work to such delicate crops as raspberries have also been developed by agricultural research establishments in Britain and the United States. But the use of the micro-chip to provide the total factory-farm tomorrow morning depends on believing the computer scientists.

Nat's farm comes, in fact, from the vision of Earl Joseph, the futurist of the American computer company Sperry-Univac (the big corporations find it imperative nowadays to have someone filling that sort of role). Joseph says that computer science could provide that farm today, without further research, and he claims that such methods of farming will be in widespread use before the year 2000. He is one of the few people with the temerity to put dates on his forecasts. Here are a few of his other bets:

By 1985. Driverless, reshapeable, uncrashable, fuel-saving, fume-reducing lorries and cars; the automated office, with 'intelligent' word-processors as the nerve-ends of the communications networks; 'smart' factories controlling their own robot-run production lines.

During the 1990s. The pocket office and the information centre worn as an ornament – the contents of the Library of Congress on your wrist; android servants, and robots directing other robots; miniaturized factories.

By 2010. The ultimate victory of miniaturization – the power of the human brain contained on one tiny chip.

Joseph is confident that microelectronics will produce those machines in that timescale. But even if Western society is ready to take such a further acceleration of change, we still lack enough skilled people to write the software (the computer programs) required to make the machine world work. Therefore, Joseph suggests adding 'three to fifteen years' to the timescale to allow time for each new development to become widespread.

But if we fail to overcome the immediate energy crisis – and also fail to develop new energy sources quickly enough as the oil really starts to run out – then Joseph believes we can deduct ten years from the later dates. His reasoning is that both the direct energy savings of microelectronics (the chips themselves consume minimal power) and the indirect savings (no heating for peopleless factories: no travelling to unnecessary offices) could hasten the shift of work and education back to the home, along the computer networks.

If that thinking from someone called a futurist seems to have ivory-tower overtones, then you might find a Delphic poll – conducted in Britain as long ago as January 1978 – more convincing. Delphic polls were devised by the American think-tank, the Rand Corporation, about ten years ago. They are simply the collected opinions of 'experts' who have answered identical questionnaires inviting them to predict the most likely date for various future events. The pooled results, corrected to eliminate extreme views, can be plotted in graphical form to show not only the most likely date but also the spread of the forecasts.

This particular questionnaire was answered by more than a thousand readers of the leading technical magazine *Computer Weekly* and its responses should therefore represent the majority verdicts of a cross-section of Britain's computer people, both in the commercial and academic worlds.

They forecast that by 1985 comprehensive information on all citizens will be held in a central, national databank. By 1987 letters will be written by talking to the typewriter. By 1992 the postal services will be in their death throes and most major government decisions will be based on computer predictions. By 1999 the average working week will have been cut to twenty hours. On only two of the twenty-one questions did the forecast date come after 2000. Those questions concerned the emergence of computers with self-awareness (thirty-two per cent said never) and 'direct connection between microprocessors and the human brain or nervous system to improve human capabilities' (nineteen per cent said never to that version of bionic man).

On the nearer future, of course, the forecasts were firmer. A solid majority said that by 1985 children will be guided through their homework by home computer terminals, and predicted that shopping services will be available in the same way. Another solid vote was that by 1990 pocket computers with radio links to computer centres will be commonplace.

But back to Jane Babbage: the third dubious element in the claim that it's all here already is the home robot which feeds at the power-point when its strength gets low. There are robots that can steer themselves through a room without precise preprogramming (they use light and touch sensors to avoid damaging the furniture), but for the robot to establish its position relative to the nearest power-point when its batteries are running down would require highly complex programming. That kind of robot, though, is one of the favourite toys of the artificial-intelligence specialists.

There we leap ahead to a long-term possibility: the creation of the self-conscious computer which thinks for itself and out-thinks us. Chapter 16 looks at that research, but here, just to illustrate the mundane possibilities of the domestic robot, is a brief sketch of one of many experiments aimed at producing a robot that learns to learn.

Alan Bond, head of the artificial intelligence unit at Queen Mary College, London University, foresees that their prototype Mark IV robot will develop into a generation of self-managing machines which will work in areas awkward for people – mines, the seabed, nuclear power stations, space. The Mark IV is battery-run on four power levels: full charge, hungry, low, and very low. While its power is above the hungry level, it roams randomly on its three wheels. As soon as the power drops, it searches with its miniature camera for a recharging point, identifiable by a light. It must find the power-point not through its programming but by trial and error – by learning. To help it, Bond and his team have painted the area around the power-point in different colours. They hope it will also learn to recognize this combination, using its four colour senses. The Mark IV also has tactile sensors to let it know when it hits another object. The robot records what it learns in the memory of its controller, a distant computer. It is supposed to use that memory to solve its next survival problem. The evidence of success is scanty so far.

The robot has apparently learned to scan for the light when it gets 'hungry' and then tentatively to trace the light path. But no more. The Bond team base their work on discoveries about the processes through which a human baby begins to learn about its surroundings. But they shy away from any inference that that necessarily indicates self-consciousness in the robot.

Enough of robots, for the moment. There are further, more fundamental objections to be made about Chapter 2. For one thing, it leaves out of account all the other, interlocking technological changes that may well take place. At the moment it seems likely that microelectronics will be the dominating technology of the next two decades. The claim has been made, even by cautious civil servants in the UK Department of Industry, that it will bring changes that have been matched in human history only by the invention of the wheel. But there are many other influences at work – not least, of course, the prospect of running out of oil and other raw materials.

There are also infant technologies which could, in the longer term, alter the rules – genetic engineering being probably the most powerful and disturbing. Further, the rate of discovery is such that the chances must be high of finding something equally fundamental just around the corner. After all, man has discovered more in the past twenty-five years than in the whole of his history before that.

A neat lesson for the over-confident forecaster was provided in one reaction to the invention of the transistor. If a single event can be nominated as the key to the development of the computer as a universal tool, then the perfecting of the transistor must be it. Yet the *New York Times,* on Thursday, 1 July 1948, carried this message: 'A device called a transistor, which has several applications in radio where a vacuum tube ordinarily is employed, was demonstrated for the first time yesterday at Bell Telephone Laboratories, 463 West Street, where it was invented.' There were three more paragraphs explaining how the bulky vacuum tube was replaced by a 'pinhead of solid semiconductive material', and that was it. What's more, the announcement was buried at the end of a column of radio programme chat. The headline was: 'New Shows on CBS Will Replace Radio Theatre During the Summer'.

But perhaps the most crucial doubt about the assumptions behind Chapter 2 lies in the human limitations on the rational management of change; not simply man's competitive inhumanity to man and the stark division between wealth and poverty in the world, but our failure to steer our progress even at a gentler pace, even on a strictly national scale – and even when there is broad consensus about where we want to go. And what do we want to achieve via microelectronics, anyway?

There are two huge assumptions about the Jane Babbage way of life: that automation will create so much wealth that we can all share more goodies; and that most people will welcome limitless leisure. Assumption A looks fine in theory, dubious in reality. The loser nations could go under in spectacular and horrific fashion; the winners could create bitter divisions between their haves and their have-nots. Assumption B is even more tenuous. Was the work ethic simply born of centuries of necessity, then tightened and deified by the demands of the First Industrial Revolution? Or is it something more fundamental, not to be dissolved in a generation or two?

That debate has been going on since the futurologists of the 1950s looked at the computer and prematurely predicted widespread automation. Now that the cheap microchip has provided the economic logic for that to happen, the evidence of what everyman actually wants is still scanty. Medical and social science research shows that unemployment can be a carrier of disease through its destruction of self-esteem. The everyday evidence for that is the sad way in which our first curiosity about people we meet is often what they do for a living.

Even if that is a removable piece of indoctrination, the problems that remain are still immense. Will most marriages survive if the partners are constantly in each other's – and their children's – company, working (or not working) at home? How do we replace the social functions of the workplace? Is there a fundamental truth behind the puritanical fear of a bread and circuses world? The standard responses to these questions are to foresee the expansion of education and community work and a vast extension of the leisure industries, so that the former factory hand or office manager retains self-esteem through wider knowledge, service to others – and becoming the local golf champion.

A more comforting version of the post-industrial society is that its most important single resource will be its human capital: the wealth of a nation will depend on the skills and knowledge of its people and how busily those are employed in providing services to the rest of the world.

Despite the various governmental and union campaigns to promote 'chip awareness', there have been surprisingly few attempts to discover what people actually think about the prospect of greater leisure. In Britain, there have been two small surveys made by National Opinion Polls. The first, in July 1978, found that seventy-five per cent of workers greatly enjoy their jobs, yet forty per cent would give up work if they could do so without loss of pay. Even thirty-eight per cent of managers voted that way, and the leisure vote rose to fifty-one per cent after the age of forty-five – 'The menopausal spurt,' according to the managing director of NOP, John Barber. But when the question was put in theoretical terms – 'Do you think it would be a good thing for society if people didn't have to work to get money but could choose whether to work or not?' – the verdict swung to eighty-three per cent against, with men (eighty-seven per cent) clinging to the work ethic more than women. To the question 'Would you like to be retrained for another job if you didn't lose money?' sixty-one per cent said no and thirty-five per cent yes; and the proportion changed to sixty-seven–thirty-two by the age of thirty-five. Fifty-eight per cent were in favour of computers taking over boring, repetitive work and twenty-nine per cent were not.

A poll conducted on an identical sampling pattern in July 1979, looked at what people hoped for from micro-electronics. The results were equally indeterminate: fifty-six per cent would like fully safe, computer-controlled cars and thirty-one per cent would not; forty-one per cent wanted voice-operated machines to do the housework and fifty-one per cent did not (among women the yes vote dropped even lower, to thirty-five per cent); and only thirty-five per cent said they would prefer to work at home. But the biggest uncertainty was on a question in the 1978 poll on whether we should have more or fewer computers: thirty-nine per cent wanted more, thirty-eight per cent fewer, and twenty-three per cent didn't know – 'A very sensible answer,' according to Barber.

Maybe – if one were sure that the twenty-three per cent were not befuddled by the computer's bogus mystique. The job of Chapter 4 is to dispel that mystique, before we move on to what the computer is actually doing to the world.

4. The chip and its origins

The digital computer understands only two signals: on or off, yes or no, nought or one. Its extraordinary dexterity comes from the vast number of those nought-or-one bits it can absorb and the speed with which it can manipulate them as the power pulses through it. The latest number-crunching machines can make 100 million calculations a second. ('Number-crunching' is one of the better pieces of computer jargon, indicating the sort of monstrous calculation that would take X men Y years.)

Those nought-and-one digits are marshalled by binary mathematics. A good illustration of how this works is to imagine a Morse code where the dots and dashes are replaced by the presence or absence of an electrical charge, the presence indicating one and the absence nought. If three noughts represent the letter S and three ones the letter O, then the distress call SOS becomes 000111000. Thus the computer can get by with only two digits – its off or on signals – instead of the ten digits used in the decimal system. But if, like me, you lack the numerate mind, it is of little consequence. The computer is no longer primarily a mathematical tool. Indeed, many computer people argue that nowadays some of the best systems analysts and programmers (the people who construct systems for a particular range of jobs and those who write the programs that direct the machine in detail) have no mathematical background.

The way in which those noughts and ones are recorded is also – in principle – simple. Take the building of a chip. Chips are made from silicon not because it is so abundant (it is a main constituent of sand) but because it is a good semi-conductor. Hence the name semi-conductor industry for the chip-making business. The term means that silicon can both conduct electricity and reject it, depending on the impurities added to the virgin material.

One small area of a chip can be doctored to deprive it of electrons while another area gets a surplus of electrons. If those two zones are separated by a third zone, the combination becomes a transistor – an electronic switch. The microscopic transistors – each chip has thousands of them – provide 'gates', which are simply on or off, to establish whether the individual signal is nought or one. Those basic pieces of yes-or-no information are called bits; when they are put together to provide a meaningful message – like our imaginary SOS – they are called bytes (computer jargon, unlike most technical vocabularies, often has a glimmer of wit about it). A byte usually consists of eight bits which, as a unit, can represent a language character or up to two decimal numerals.

Today's so-called microcomputers are built from a small collection of two sorts of chips: a microprocessor that does the work and memory devices that hold and organize the information. But the computer on a single chip, combining storage and processing, has now emerged. It is those real microcomputers that look like becoming universal components – the nuts and bolts of the post-Industrial Revolution. One irony of that prospect is that the youthful trade of computer programming could itself become redundant. Many computer scientists see the chip computer as a key to automating the mechanical aspects of the job of instructing the computer, leaving just the pure thinking, so that people without specialist knowledge can use the computer directly to solve problems.

Through the 1970s the basic cost of computing power dropped forty per cent a year – every year – as circuitry was packed ever more tightly on the chip. In the 1960s, about seventy per cent of the cost of putting together a commercial computer system went on the machinery and thirty per cent on the programs and the people to run it. Those proportions have already been reversed, and the process will accelerate further in the 1980s. One of the standard boasts of the business goes like this : if the motor industry had moved at the speed of the computer industry, then a Rolls-Royce today would cost about five dollars; it would do three million miles to the gallon, and you could put five limousines on your fingertip.

The justification for that boast can be summarized in one comparison : a microprocessor chip today does roughly the same amount of work as one of the early, elephantine post-war computers.

Take ENIAC, built at Pennsylvania University in 1946. That one covered 3000 cubic feet, weighed 30 tons, and consumed 140 kilowatts of power. The microprocessor occupies 0·011 of a cubic foot, weighs a gramme or two, and uses 2·5 watts. And, being a machine with no moving parts, it is about 10,000 times more reliable. The microprocessor is already so complex that you have to take it on trust : it is impossible to test it fully to make sure it will perform all the millions of functions of which it is capable.

We are nowhere near the limits of miniaturization. The chip will become still cheaper and still faster (as the messages find even shorter routes to travel). Already the circuitry is so closely drawn that the problem of electrons leaking from the lines has to be faced. Some physicists say it will soon become possible – perhaps by 1985 – to put the power of a big mid-1960s computer on to a single part about the size of a matchhead.

Already in orthodox silicon technology more than 64,000 bits (equivalent to around a thousand English language words) are stored on one fragile fragment an eighth of an inch across and less than half a millimetre thick – slim enough to pass through the eye of a needle. Viewed under a microscope, those chips look like the ultimate in railway marshalling yards; and the lines that carry the messages around can be thinner than a thirtieth of the width of a human hair. The information they hold can be released at a rate of five bits every one millionth of a second. That speed represents, in theory at least, reading the Bible, Authorized Version, in $7\frac{1}{2}$ seconds. (And it's a minor sign of the times that I did that sum in a few seconds on a Japanese calculator no bigger than a fist-hidden bridge hand.)

Yet a branch technology – the bubble memory – is already beating that: it can hold a million bits on a chip. In a bubble memory, minute pockets of magnetism (the bubbles) are created in the semi-conducting material. When prodded by a magnetic field they move along pathways and, as they pass fixed points, the presence or absence of the bubbles is recorded as the basic nought-or-one bits. Under the microscope the bubbles look like a family of rabbits scuttling through their burrow.

A crucial advantage of the bubble memory is that it retains its information when the power is switched off. It is one of the techniques that will, sooner or later, take over the job of storing computer data from such bulkier, slower devices as magnetic tapes and discs. The million-bit bubble memory is already on sale. But the research labs are playing with bubbles that would provide 100 million bits (the contents of the Bible three times over) on one square inch of garnet crystals. Those bubbles are only four-tenths of a micron in diameter (and a micron is one 10,000th of a centimetre). The problem still to be solved is the creation of circuitry small enough to carry them.

One solution may be to shrink the pathways with a laser beam. This has been done experimentally, reducing pathways from a width of sixteen microns to seven. It works like this: a laser can heat a small region of material to a high temperature so rapidly that the surrounding material stays cool. As the laser scans the material, the regions that have been heated cool so quickly that their high-temperature structure is frozen in. Thus a sample can be heated precisely to a temperature at which a known change in crystal structure occurs – then cooled so rapidly that that high-temperature structure stays, even though it does not normally exist at room temperature.

But that's for the future: the possible computers of 1990 get a chapter to themselves. The content of the routine, cheap chip of today is awesome enough. Memory chips that store the information are less complex in structure but more tightly packed than microprocessors. Therefore they provide the best illustration of what can be contained in that microscopic world. If you magnified one just enough to distinguish the smallest lines with the naked eye then you would have produced a square about the size of a standard carpet – the sides would be ten feet long. Nowadays that actually happens, in a fashion.

In the chip's cruder days, designs were hand-made, drawn large-scale on boards, then photographed down and down to chip size. (The original vividly coloured drawings, with the designers' signatures in the corner, are often displayed like works of art in the lobbies of American semi-conductor compaines: one firm has even produced a coffee-table book of them.) But today that would be impossible in detail – you would need a drawing cast of thousands. So the computer takes over. The designer draws what he wants on the computer screen, using an instrument known as a light pencil that reacts electronically with the screen; then he tells the computer where to place that part in the grand design and, maybe, repeat it scores of times in scores of places, with scores of connections.

The computer will then print a coloured drawing of its solution in human-scale strips; and those strips would make up the imaginary carpet. In fact, you can do without the carpet. The designer can call on to the screen the totality or any part of it – and in three dimensions, for the chip's structure, thin as it is, can still go down to ten layers or more in coatings and the building of gates and lines.

The computer has also become essential in manufacturing the chips – the old science fiction theme of computers creating computers has been reality for several years. To explain that, we need to go back to the beginning.

The beginning is a block of purest silicon. It looks like a German sausage but has the weight of a cosh. The block is sliced into razor-thin discs, called wafers, and the chips are made in clusters on those wafers. Up to 250 chips can be built on a wafer three inches across. With the demand for chips increasing, four-inch wafers have been introduced and experiments are being made with five-inch – not so easy and obvious as it might sound, because of the fragility of the material.

The chips are etched on the wafers by a method derived from the photolithographic methods used to reproduce photographs. The design is reduced to microscopic size, then transferred to the silicon through 'masks'. Those masks control the etching – the uncovered parts of the mask allow the corresponding parts of the chip to be chemically nibbled, and the covered parts then remain raised on the chip, reproducing the design. That etching is the core of a series of coating and baking processes which can involve more than fifty stages for the latest VLSI (very large scale integration) chips.

The chip-making process itself illustrates one of the toughest lessons about its own product: anything microelectronic introduced today is, by definition, already out of date. The circuitry is now so tightly packed that the computer has to disgorge the design details on to the mask via electron beams. Electron-beam cutters are also beginning to be used to bombard the chip itself with electrons, as one way of eliminating the already inadequate chemical etching methods.

Chip-making also illustrates the cross-fertilization in high technology. Just as the original chemical process was adapted from the photolithography of the printing industry, so might the development of solar energy help to improve chip production. The wafers on which silicon solar cells (the basic unit of solar heat conversion) are founded are broadly similar to the chip wafers, though the solar cell is a much simpler product, with one cell occupying the whole of a wafer. The research labs of one of the biggest microelectronics companies, Motorola, in Phoenix, Arizona, have devised square wafers for their solar cells which, of course, offer a greater total area to the sun than the orthodox circular ones. More impressively, they are experimenting with laser-led techniques which provide the silicon in long sheets.

A chip factory is, in fact, called a wafer fabrication plant, because its end product is the wafer with the chips on board. Those wafers are then usually flown to the cheap labour areas of the Far East for the chips to be separated and mounted individually – ready to be connected to, and work for, the coarser world outside. A wafer fabrication plant bears no resemblance to the factories of old. It is a collection of quiet, sterile, lab-like rooms.

The production workers – at least nine out of ten of whom will be women – look like surgeons, in white coats, helmets, gloves, and overshoes. They work in an atmosphere filtered to such an extent that each cubic foot of air is supposed to contain less than a hundred specks of matter – and none of those more than a 20,000th of a centimetre wide; the temperature variation is contained within two degrees; and, in some cases, the workers vacuum the floor before they start. All that filtering, dehumidifying and double dressing is caused by the fact that one speck of dust can make nonsense of a microscopic integrated circuit. A few years ago it was not uncommon for a production line to produce fifty duds for one honest chip. Today, most firms claim a success rate of fifty to sixty per cent, though that can fall to fifteen per cent on the new lines devoted to VLSI. More than thirty per cent of production costs can go into testing that the chips work.

Automation is still advancing fast in chip production. In one of the latest factories, at Stuttgart in West Germany, the fifty or so stages involved in building the chips have, in effect, been cut to eight, because many of the computer-run tools can handle several operations. The silicon wafers are floated around that plant on glass-tunnelled railways of dust-cleared air, untouched by human hand or mechanical contrivance. As each chip-bearing disc is carried from department to department, process to process, on its cushion of air, its progress is charted in a central control room, both in moving red lights on a wall map and on computer display screens.

That factory demonstrates one of the oddities of the chip business. It belongs to International Business Machines (IBM), an American company which probably makes more chips than anybody else – yet it does not sell any. IBM dominates the computer business – it makes more than sixty per cent of the world's computers – and it needs all the chips it can make, and more, to put into its own machines.

However, most of the chip-making is still done by the semi-conductor industry proper, and in one small corner of California: a peninsular strip about thirty miles by ten in Santa Clara County, along the south-western shore of San Francisco Bay. It is called, inevitably, Silicon Valley, and there the semi-conductor industry first gathered itself in 1958.

The industry was born from the early work in solid-state physics and it still lives by innovation. The scientist as businessman is the rule not the exception. Semi-conductor people are a young, vivid breed. They thrive on a double drug – the inventive fascination of an awesome technology and the tightrope of cut-throat, research-based competition. The obvious parallel is the professional sportsman: you find the same closed-world camaraderie, where the performers talk with glowing respect of their rivals' talents. In Silicon Valley you can see a fresh-faced PhD, who looks like a newcomer to the sixth form, running a multi-million-dollar production line; top management eating in the canteen and tending to talk more technical than financial shop; and designers and engineers from rival companies exchanging solutions to problems on the golf course or in the cool of the bars.

The Valley presents a vigorous if vulgar face. Semiconductor companies jostle each other alongside the freeways, their plants often separated only by the equally crowded company parking lots and the garishly-signalled motels. The glossy company buildings are as low as the landscape (because sites were cheap when many of them were built around a decade ago), but the flat monotony is relieved by the long, lush, leafy avenues of middle-class homes, which branch from the highways; by the western horizon of shaggy hills, which leads to the Pacific; and, of course, by the cosmetic of the Californian sunshine.

The competitive togetherness of Silicon Valley has never been absolute. From the early days there has been semiconductor manufacture elsewhere in the United States, notably in Texas, home of the biggest semi-conductor company, Texas Instruments; but Santa Clara County is still the world centre for chip-making. Though perhaps not for long. That status is being eroded, first by the increase in demand as the chip begins to take a wider role as a component in virtually all industries; then by the challenge from Japanese chip firms and probably – from Europe as well in the 1980s; then by the problem of finding space for expansion in that narrow peninsula as housing and land costs rise; but, above all, by the intensifying competition for talent.

The semi-conductor industry – like the computer business – is getting too big for its original boots and is desperately short of skilled and experienced people. Secret signing-on fees of more than 20,000 dollars are reckoned to be commonplace in the middle ranks of the Silicon Valley transfer market – though the firms that tell you this always add that they never pay under-cover money themselves. Intel, the company that first launched the microprocessor and which has grown from nothing to an annual turnover of 400 million dollars in ten years, would like to take on twenty-five per cent more graduates than it can find. Gerry Parker, the company's director of technical development, says that nearly half his graduate staff of physicists and engineers – and about seventy per cent of the PhDs – come from Taiwan, Israel, India, and Pakistan, in that order. Most of them were educated at American universities, yet suitable native American graduates are apparently hard to find.

By the summer of 1979 the US industry was nearly six months behind in coping with the sudden expansion in orders: by 1980 there was something of a world chip famine and the latest chips made in Japan were taking nearly a third of the American home market.

Thus the swings of history could make the link between the chip and the original Chinese abacus of 2600 years ago less tenuous than it appears. The progress of the calculating machine has, in fact, paralleled most of the other developments that have reshaped the way we live: a barely rising curve for many hundreds of years, then a lift in the seventeenth and eighteenth centuries, a much steeper slope in the nineteenth century, and a virtually vertical takeoff in the second half of the twentieth century.

A number of mechanical calculators appeared in the seventeenth century, but the true grandfather of the modern computer was Charles Babbage, an English mathematician. With government aid, he built his 'Difference Engine' in

1822. That machine produced the first reliable tables of life expectancy, which were used for the next fifty years. Then, in 1833, he expanded his ideas into a machine that would automate the whole process of calculation, his 'Analytical Engine'. The government got cold feet at that stage and withdrew its support, but Babbage, who was then Lucasian Professor of Mathematics at Cambridge, devoted the rest of his life to producing his universal digital calculator. He had thirty-eight years left, but he never made it: the precision engineering required was beyond the technology of his day. But the notes he left showed that his 'engine' contained (in mechanical terms) all the elements of today's electronic computers. There was a store to hold the information, before and after processing; a 'mill' of gears and wheels to do the actual calculating; a control unit to transfer information between store and mill and check what was going on; and input and output devices to enter the data and display the results of the machine's work.

Since the digital computer is now supreme, I will sweepingly ignore the advances towards analog computing (that is, measuring in flows rather than in separate digits). This allows us to jump to the 1880s, when one H. Hollerith of the United States Census Bureau invented a method of storing information in holes punched in cards. His techniques were used in the US census of 1890 and the British census of 1911 – and, more importantly, were taken up by International Business Machines. That was IBM's headstart. Today it is one of the world's most powerful companies.

Electro-mechanical machines that read those punched cards were the business computers of the 1930s. The demands of code-breaking and ballistic measurement in the Second World War encouraged the emergence of the electronic computer and the programming techniques that made it adaptable. If one had to select two names from that seminal period they might be Alan Turing, a British mathematician whose theoretical work in the 1930s and code-breaking work in the 1940s helped to lay the foundations; and the American mathematician John Von Neumann, who produced, post-war, the vital concept of storing programs in the computer itself rather than laboriously feeding them in. That period also began computer people's hideous habit of devising acronyms. Those computers of the late 1940s and early 1950s, massive machines relying on thousands of bulky vacuum tubes, included the ENIAC, the EDVAC, the SEAC and the UNIVAC in the US, and the EDSAC at Cambridge University.

But Manchester University claims to have run the first stored-program computer, more suitably dubbed the Mark I. That achievement, on 21 June 1948, was the breakthrough to the general-purpose computer and thus a core event in the creation of the new industry. A government contract was given to the Manchester firm of Ferranti, in November 1948, to make a production version of the Mark I, and that is claimed to be the first commercially available computer, marginally ahead of the American UNIVAC. The Ferranti Mark I was called the blue pig by the maintenance engineers but the Manchester Electronic Computer (never MEC) in the sales brochures.

By that time the transistor had been introduced, leading, of course, to the huge expansion in the uses of the computer, via microelectronics, and to the rise of the semiconductor industry. The first transistor was made at Bell Telephone laboratories on 23 December 1974, and publicly demonstrated six months later. In 1956 the leaders of the Bell team – William Shockley, John Bardeen and Walter Houser Brattain – received the Nobel prize in physics. Their application of the understanding of how electrons in metals are free to move and conduct electricity was rooted in the work in quantum mechanics which got seriously underway in the 1920s. Brattain recently said of the Bell work: 'The transistor came about because fundamental knowledge had developed to a stage where human minds could understand phenomena that had been observed for a long time. In the case of a device with such important consequences to technology, it is noteworthy that a breakthrough came from work dedicated to the understanding of fundamental physical phenomena, rather than a cut-and-try method of producing a useful device.'

Shockley was one of the founders of Silicon Valley. In 1955 he set up the first semi-conductor company there, in his home town, Palo Alto. His reputation attracted a talented team, and in 1957 eight of that team – all originally from the older electronic firms in the east – started their own company with the backing of Fairchild Camera and Instrument Corporation. Fairchild Semi-conductors was the real launcher of Silicon Valley. From it sprang the development of the integrated circuit, the electronic device with no moving parts, into chips containing hundreds, then thousands, of transistors. More than forty semi-conductor companies have been formed by scientists who once worked at Fairchild, though that company has now lost its top place and has become a subsidiary of a wider electronics group.

The next key step was to turn those collections of integrated circuits into a machine that could be called a computer in itself: the microprocessor. The man who did that is Dr Ted Hoff, who in December 1979 received the Stuart Ballantine Medal from the Franklin Institute for his invention. Hoff joined the microelectronics company Intel when it began in Silicon Valley in 1968. He was then thirty-one. A year later he proposed the architecture of the first microprocessor and that went on sale as the Intel 4004, in 1971.

While microelectronics was being born in California, Britain was falling behind the US in the (then) distantly related world of computers. In pre-chip 1953, magnetic core storage (working on the same basic principle as the later bubble memories) was the next jump ahead: IBM took it and established a two-year lead.

Today the US still dominates both industries, but Japan is catching up fast and Western Europe is taking a firmer stake. Trailing behind IBM, like sparrows pecking after the pigeon, is a cluster of American multinational computer companies. But Europe has only one major, independent contender in that world league: International Computers (ICL), a British company formed in 1965 from a chain of mergers.

IBM's dominance has created two sub-industries: the IBM-watchers (consultants and analysts who give the rest of computing's global village their version of what the colossus will do next) and the IBM-copiers, computer manufacturers who make machines that are 'plug compatible' – that is, they work in the same way as IBM computers do, so they can replace IBM machines or work alongside them. That is another absurdity of the computer business: the leading companies make machines that will work only with their own machines, not anybody else's. So if a customer wants a computer from A to do one job but a computer from B to do another, he has to spend a lot of extra money to make them 'compatible'. That makes him think twice before he tries another shop.

The fierce competition of the computer manufacturers was showing slight signs of settling into the outwardly staid respectability of other big businesses when along came the second-phase expansion of the chip's capabilities in the mid-1970s. This has begun to shrink the top end of the mainstream manufacturers' market, because customers don't want so many big, central computers when they can build a network of little ones; equally, the bottom end of their market is being increasingly nibbled by the companies specializing in minicomputers; they, in turn, are being got at from below by a swarm of new or reinvigorated companies making still cheaper microcomputers and word-processors.

On top of that, the chip has hastened the convergence of

the previously largely separate computer, telecommunications, and general electronic industries. Now everybody is jostling everybody else. Computer companies are racing into communications; telecommunications groups are sharpening their computer expertise in order to offer the totally automated office themselves; meanwhile, in the even faster-spreading market for consumer products born of or revolutionized by the chip, the Japanese are having it much their own way.

And the people who started it all – the semi-conductor firms – are themselves beset by bizarre new problems. World demand for the chip seems certain to go on rising through the 1980s, whatever the economic climate; yet some manufacturers say that the chip business is becoming so precarious that no one will be able to survive by making chips alone and there will have to be more vertical integration, with firms providing chip-run products as well. The only new entrants are the government-backed enterprises of Japan and Western Europe. No entrepreneurs are tempted to plunge into a volatile industry that demands an entrance fee of 100 million dollars and more. That is why governments (and – increasingly – the big multinational corporations) are moving into the business through the side door, to ensure their share of this core industrial component. There are a number of long-term doubters to be found in Silicon Valley. Their arguments run like this:

Probably no other industry owes so much to pure science – and to continued research. At each successive stage of boosting and shrinking the product, the firm that has got in first with a sound design has taken the choicest pickings from the limited lifespan of that particular chip style. That firm could go into mass production before its rivals; thus cut production costs – and then cut prices to destroy the competition. They call that rat race the learning curve.

Now the process is accelerating once again. This means, some argue, that the industry is returning to the atmosphere of its even riskier pioneering days in the 1950s when (in the words of a Fairchild veteran, Lester Hogan) new technologies were tumbling out of the laboratories every few months. Virtually every new development today has its successor not only being designed but existing in hardware around the laboratories; and every new device costs more to evolve – and then more to make – than did its less complex predecessor. The cost of setting up a new production line has quadrupled in five years.

What is more, some people fear that the pace of scientific advance will actually cut demand. Despite the spreading of the chip into consumer products, telecommunications, and factory production lines, the semi-conductor business still relies overwhelmingly on one industry to buy its chips – the computer industry. Today's minicomputers are essentially little more than a few circuit boards packed with chips. If one chip tomorrow will do the work of twenty today, then who will buy the other nineteen? And will the chips get so good that few users will want half the vast number-crunching capability they will offer?

But the economic arguments about the speed at which we are creating the Jane Babbage world – arguments that go beyond those business doubts to the roots of national politics and the international balance of power – must wait a while. First, let's see how far we are along the Babbage road at the beginning of the 1980s.

5. Why information is power

The Japanese saw it first (in national terms, at least) and called it the Information Society. In their formal fashion they produced a blueprint to build it at the start of the 1970s. The immediate commercial triumph of that national policy is to be seen in high-street shops around the world. The theory of the Information Society is, you remember, that information will become the key resource, demoting the traditional production factors such as capital, labour, land, and raw materials.

Later, the French found the word for the broad range of chip-related machines and skills that has begun to build such a post-industrial world. They called it informatics. The message of informatics is that rapid and wide access to information is power. And one of the neatest illustrations of the truth of that message can be found in the sewers. The sewers and water mains of most English cities were constructed in Victorian times. For more than a century those sub-cities of pipes have muddled along. Millions of nasty man-hours and many millions of pounds have been wasted simply because no one knew what was going on down there. Now, thanks to the chip, the area water authorities of Britain are finding out – cheaply.

In the West of England, the Wessex Water Authority has spent about £50,000 since 1977 on surveying water flows and pressures in a five per cent sample spread across its region. That survey immediately saved £700,000 in capital expenditure, and by the autumn of 1979 the authority was estimating that the savings in energy consumption would soon be running at £150,000 to £200,000 a year. The capital saving came from scrapping – or, at least, postponing for a long while – a plan to build an £800,000 reservoir. The survey illuminated a better option : to supply that particular increase in demand from elsewhere in the region, at a cost of £100,000. The energy savings come mainly from adjusting water pressures to real needs. One of the most dramatic examples was at Swanage, in Dorset, where the night pressure was reduced by half – saving about £3000 a year on electricity in that small town alone.

Those revolutionary increases in management efficiency come solely from accurate and fast information, not from direct automation. The water industry in many countries is moving rapidly in direct automation, too – the other dimension of greater economy and quality of supply. Electronic instruments that have increased accuracy of measurement a hundredfold are also being used to control the flows along the networks, as well as at source in rivers and reservoirs. But, in Britain, the water industry has tended to rest on its Victorian laurels; now it has to tackle the problem of the ageing sewers. Chip-controlled remote TV cameras – drawn through the sewers on skids, and recording with their pictures the time and the distance covered – have exposed all the expected horrors : huge cracks, tree roots intruding, branch pipes poked crudely into main sewers. The 1980s method of tackling those nineteenth-century relics is typified by two rooms in the Wessex authority's headquarters in Bristol : the big, antiseptic regional control centre on the ground floor and the appropriately small microcomputer room, hidden in a corner of the second floor.

The main clue to the future is in the little room. There a microcomputer system has built a databank of all useful information about the water supply and sewage systems in the region, including four thousand maps, pinpointing every pipe and hydrant, with full technical details; an interpretative system for faults reported by the recording instruments – with predictions of their impact; a directory of towns and villages, with details of the people to be contacted in emergencies, from duty water officers to district council officials; the current state of water storage in the impounding reservoirs and the historical pattern of fluctuations of supply and (holiday area) demand throughout the year; the same sort of information about the weather; and a directory of chemicals, illustrating what needs to be done if, say, a crashed tanker's load gets into the sewers.

Thus the system can be used both for planning work and emergency decisions. It will spill its information in statistical, map, or multicoloured graph form; and it has been designed for use by people unaccustomed to computers – advice appears on the screen to advise the user at every stage of his search for decision-forming information.

The roomful of equipment cost less than £40,000 and the microcomputer itself was, inevitably, the cheapest item. Most of the money went on data storage and the digital plotter that converts maps into computer data. (That plotter, by the way, is so precise that the computer complains about, then corrects, the slight distortions that appear when maps are copied.)

The regional controller (one man monitors the whole region, covering five counties, from 5 p.m. till 8.30 a.m.) can, in emergency, rally his information in seconds. Previously, he had to dig into card-index cabinets and check duty rosters. Now not only does that information appear on his computer screen in a coordinated bundle; he also has the statistics and the calculating power to adjust water pressures precisely and quickly if a main bursts.

The chip's flexibility has taken the computer into a tighter spot than the sewer: the coalface. Microcomputers began to control coal-cutters in 1980, and this must be one of the toughest environments the chip has encountered so far – embedded in a machine, twenty feet long and weighing twenty tons, which shakes and rattles like a punk band as it advances at four miles an hour along a claustrophobic corridor of dust and heat.

This further step towards the automated mine is being tried by the British National Coal Board. The coal-cutter is studded with sensors which probe the state of the rock and coal around it, measuring the natural gamma radiation. The information from those sensors is collected and analysed by microcomputers buried in the bodywork; and the boss computer of the team uses that information to order the cutter's next moves. Thus the cutting head will match the undulations of the coal seam, always biting coal and never rock, and relieving the miner of the awesome task of directing the machine when he is twenty feet away from the action.

That miniature computer network within the coal-cutter is part of a wider network of microcomputers down the mine – controlling coal clearance and preparation, monitoring pit ventilation and underground machinery, and all reporting continually to a surface control station.

The broad principle of the computer network is the same wherever it goes. Microelectronics has simply made it go further, faster. The chips down the sewers and the mines are doing the same job as the airline booking networks which have been working for years, handling seat reservations in 'real time' (that is, making immediate decisions) for 250 airlines world-wide; or the financial network that links 500 banks in fifteen countries; or an individual company's database, dealing with personal records or financial analyses and disgorging its information on to computer terminals thousands of miles from head office; or a police computer from which an officer on the beat can in seconds extract details of a suspect via his radio; or a computer-run supermarket checkout, which tells a central computer what you and thousands of others buy – as you buy it – so that stocks can be replenished quickly.

But the chip is bringing one particularly significant change to these networks: it is providing more power to the outposts – distributed processing, in the jargon. A desktop computer terminal today can do a lot more than simply exchange information with its parent computer. It can store chunks of that information and do a lot of work on it itself. And its capacity is increasing all the time.

The obvious question then becomes: why have a big central computer at all? Why not a series of small computers, all holding the same information, all keeping each other informed of what they are doing and immediately telling each other how the common stock of information needs to be changed in consequence? That's already happening, on a smallish scale.

There's a good example of it on NATO's battle exercise fields in West Germany. The British Army claims to be the first to use battlefront computers, and it has decided – after two years of prototype development and trials – to entrust all the operational information of 1st Corps, Rhine Army, to a network of thirty-two mini-computers. Those computers are spread around camouflaged tents and trucks hidden in woods. As the battlefront shifts, the computers are trundled across country, while a back-up system fills in. Within half an hour of the roving headquarters re-settling, they are in action again, receiving and sending information by coded radio, and linked by cable to their display terminals in the tents.

The first stage of the system (called 'Wavell') has been on trial with 2nd Armoured Division. It is now being spread from Corps headquarters, through divisional headquarters, down to computers carried in task-force armoured vehicles. Details of troop movements and intelligence reports, keyboarded into the system in battlefield conditions, will be available on all computer screens throughout the Corps within seconds. At the same time, each of the isolated computers will update the identical databanks, changing equipment and troop totals, readjusting positions. Thus commanders, high and low, can base their decisions on facts minutes, not hours, old – and they don't have to waste time on the field phones. Bubble memories are being introduced to hold the information and each of the computers will then have a store of about five million words.

That information is organized in pages of pre-defined formats. For instance, an analysis of enemy strength can be displayed in constantly updated statistical tables – so many tanks in X and Y positions and commanded (we think) by Z – or in crude map form, showing their front-line dispositions.

'Wavell' was at first confined to intelligence work, but its storage capacity and processing power is now being used by the engineers, the artillery, and the logisticians as well. One of those side uses is what the army calls real estate management: the placement of units, and their logistic support, down to bath units, can be plotted on the screen in kilometre squares.

That, then, is one form of distributed processing and (jargon again) database management. Whether that will become the popular way for organizations, big and small, to work is a matter of debate in the computer community.

One of the arguments for the continued need for central computers in networks much bigger than 'Wavell' is the problem called the deadly handshake. Airline bookings provide an example. A travel agent in New York books a seat from New York to London. It is the last seat on that flight tonight. Within the same minute an airport desk in Toronto books the same seat. Imagine that clash repeated a hundredfold in a complexity of interlocking bookings, some for journeys covering three flights by different airlines in different countries.

The system's duplicated databases would not catch up in time and double reservations would proliferate in a chain of false decisions – the deadly handshakes. Therefore, airline bookings depend on powerful, fast-working central computers, taking reservations in sequence – central decision-making.

Computer networks spread through the 1970s in a variety of shapes and sizes and for a multitude of uses. Perhaps the most spectacular are the international services which offer their customers, by plugging a terminal into the phone line, the processing power of a battery of big computers on the other side of the world. This is called time-sharing, because hundreds of different organizations can share the use of the computers at the same time. These services are used both by smaller companies, which cannot afford such computer power themselves, and by big multinational groups, which find them an economical support to their own private networks.

Thus information about your pay or your credit-worthiness may at this moment be bouncing back and forth around the world by ocean cable or space satellite; though that information should be surrounded by far greater security than if it were stuffed in a filing cabinet.

For nearly two years Guy's Hospital in London used the biggest of these networks – Mark III, run by General Electric in the United States – for its patients' records, including para-medical details like laboratory tests and electro-cardiograms. Mark III has nearly 50,000 customers, served by three computer centres, two in America, one in Amsterdam. The hospital had computer terminals contacting the US centres by phone line, via Amsterdam, and its methods illustrate how strong computer security can be – when trouble is taken.

An operator at the hospital's terminal first needed the phone number of the Amsterdam centre. Then he needed to key in the hospital's code number, then a catalogue number, then a user number. Even then he could not reach the required information, because the data at the computer centres was held in two halves. Medical details were stored in one part of the system and the name and address of the individual concerned in another. A program password was needed to link the two. The hospital also ran regular checks to ensure that no information was garbled en route.

But note the past tense. Since November 1979, all that has been put on to one minicomputer at Guy's Hospital – and that computer serves two other hospitals as well, handling the records of about 30,000 patients a year. Such is the speed of change in the computer world. Presumably, as compact computer capability becomes still cheaper, the big time-sharing services will dwindle, as will the computer bureaux that do the same sort of work at local level.

But another type of international network (in which some of the time-sharing services have an interest) is just starting to grow. That is the specialized information bank. It is possible so far to get instant access to about twenty million abstracts of scientific, technical, and professional papers from such banks.

In the 1970s the computer has contributed to giving us more knowledge – in quantity if not in quality – than in any previous decade. In this context, it's worth re-emphasizing a point made in Chapter 4: the graph of knowledge gained, rising ever more steeply through three centuries, is now approaching the vertical – more new information in twenty years than in the previous 5000. About a thousand new book titles are published each day throughout the world and the total of all printed knowledge is doubling every eight years.

In the commerce and government of an increasingly complex industrialized world, the computer has enormously broadened the flood of information – and helped to channel and control that flood. Similarly, in science and technology, the computer has become an essential aid to solving problems – and, through the information banks, an essential aid in tracing who has solved what problems, where and when.

However, as databanks get bigger and their use spreads

beyond the computer professionals, the problem of pin-pointing what you want becomes greater. Even the elaborate cross-indexing of commercial and technical databanks can leave the amateur keyboard-user with the suspicion that he has not grasped the whole. One solution is a structure of pre-defined chunks of information, presented on the screen as separate pages, with each page offering pointers to the following pages, as in the British Army's 'Wavell' system. But in wider use (as we shall see in Chapter 6) that, too, can become confusing.

The Massachusetts Institute of Technology has found a garish answer. It has worked on the theory that these problems are often caused by people being accustomed to storing and finding information in spatial terms – rows of filing cabinets or shelves of books. Therefore it has devised Dataland, which puts the electronic library into three dimensions. The Dataland user sits in a room surrounded by colour TV sets with stereo sound, and he uses a joystick to navigate himself through the data.

But in time, as computers get still faster, the machines should be able to adapt themselves to the odd ways in which our individual minds work. Already there are computer systems that can answer the vaguest of questions, by leaning much more heavily on the speed of the machine itself than on the logical structure of human programming instructions. In essence, those systems find the answer by reading almost everything they contain – every one of millions of words, like looking individually at every grain of sand on the shore.

An example is a system constructed by the ICL company. It is called CAFS 800 (an acronym for content adressable file store) and its prototype is being used to run directory enquiries at two English phone exchanges. Twelve terminals at the exchanges are linked to a computer several hundred miles away. That computer holds six million directory entries – previously recorded in sixty volumes –

yet phone operators find the answers appearing on their screens within two seconds, on average. Even when the caller says he wants the number of a Reid, Reed, Read, or Reade, whose initials, he thinks, are C.P. or E.P. and who lives in St Ive or one of the St Ives, the possibles can be listed in a few seconds.

Most information retrieval systems work through an elaborate index. The programming instructs the computer to look in certain files and to tie together the relevant information from those different sources; and, in those blocks of data, drawn from storage discs, only one item in a thousand might be relevant. So a double bottleneck can be created, first along the data highway transferring the information from disc to computer, then in the computer itself as it has to scan all that data.

CAFS 800 dodges those bottlenecks. The central computer tells the CAFS sub-system what it wants by a simple 'selection specification' (say, the description of a person or a name) and a 'retrieval expression' (give address and credit rating of that person, for instance). CAFS can then use the speed offered by microelectronics to hunt right through a databank, simply plucking out the relevant pieces as it goes, before it bothers the central computer. But that could still take as long as fifteen to twenty seconds. Therefore, normally CAFS compromises by using a third 'look there' instruction, using a simple version of indexing.

It is easy to envisage the next stage – no indexing at all; no need, however huge the databank, to relate your mind to the way the thing works, and every vagary of your memory pandered to. Let me, selfishly, gave an example of the advantages of that from a journalist's viewpoint. A reporter is hurriedly gathering an account of an oil tanker collision. He has ten minutes left before deadline. He has a tentative memory of a similar collision five years before, which pointed some relevant lessons about sea lanes.

He tells the computer to find anything in the newspaper's

editions of five years ago which mentions oil tankers, sea lanes, and collision, and (afterthought) English Channel. The computer then reads every word of every issue of the paper in that year, looking for a report that contains all those words; if just one word of the combination is missing from a particular report, the computer will ignore that report. Within a few seconds it will be offering the reporter an account of the official enquiry into that collision five years ago. If the reporter's memory was vague about the year it would take a bit longer.

That search still has some structure to it – the year. But with the expanding capabilities of microelectronic storage, replacing cumbersome discs and tapes, even that sort of restraint might become counter-productive. It might become actually quicker, at some time in the 1980s or 1990s, to let the computer roam through the lot – every word in every issue of the newspaper for, perhaps, a decade.

Possibilities like that unveil a division in the computer world. Those who embrace the prospect of the computer becoming everyman's everyday assistant say that that could be done tomorrow. Those wedded to the old-fashioned computer world of intricate software and central control say it will not happen. This division appears even more strongly in attitudes to the development of computers that talk and computers that 'understand' human speech (of which much more later). Even the youngest profession has its Luddites.

If, after that brief glimpse of networks and databanks, you remain unconvinced that information itself is wealth, here is a more primitive, personal example. I carry with me a tattered blue notebook. It is vital to my work as a journalist, because it contains a few thousand names and phone numbers of government officials and academics, industrialists and trade union leaders, concerned with high technology in various parts of the world. If my wallet were stuffed with hundreds of pounds (it never is), I would rather have it stolen than lose the notebook. Within a few years, it should be possible to replace that notebook with an attachment to my wrist watch.

Raw information, as well as wisdom-based knowledge, has, of course, long been a saleable commodity. Trade directories and railway timetables are obvious examples. What the computer has done is to extend prodigiously the amount of information we can use, the speed at which we can locate it, and the extent to which we can correlate it.

But for that to produce the sort of world envisaged for Jane Babbage, back in Chapter 2, those networks have to extend to the home. That, too, has begun ...

6. How TV was re-invented

The process of bringing computer networks into the home has begun through an invention called viewdata, which originated in the British Post Office. Viewdata is a computer-run public information service. It turns the home television set into a combination of instant newspaper, mail-order house, encyclopaedia, message service, consumer guide, booking office and professional advice centre. It can be used as a symbol of the transition to the post-industrial society because it epitomizes the prizes and the problems offered by the computer in the 1980s.

The service, being extended across Britain by the Post Office, is based on a series of computer centres, each with identical databanks, updated minute by minute. Customers in home or office contact those databanks via the phone line, though they don't have to lift the phone receiver. They use instead a hand-held keypad with numbers, like a pocket calculator, to summon to their TV screen the pages of information they want.

In theory, the number of pages available could be limit-less. In fact, the total was just under 200,000 in the spring of 1980, and the aim then was to increase the storage capacity to 500,000 within two years. That information, presented in coloured graphs and diagrams as well as words, is supplied by about 150 organizations – governmental, commercial, industrial, social, professional, advertising and publishing. (Publishing predominates on the basis of seizing a precautionary share of the new competition.)

You can think of those thousands of pages as a forest,

with each of the organizations supplying the information as owning some of the trees, though that's an analogy frowned upon by viewdata purists. You start at the base of the tree, and, by following the instructions that appear on each page, you punch numbers on the keypad to climb the tree, page by page, till you reach the final branch that contains the detailed information you want. You can also, like a super-charged squirrel, leap from tree to tree, through cross-reference guides which the pages give to related subjects. For instance, if you were using viewdata to look up flights to Glasgow, that page might also tell you how to consult a Glasgow hotel guide in another part of the viewdata forest.

Fine in theory, but Post Office research has shown that people can get lost that way. Using the keypad alone produces an average 'hit rate' of only 80 per cent. That has led to the birth of one of the several viewdata sub-industries: the publishing of guides to the system which enable you to move straight to the page you want. There are several fat guides available, some general, some for business information only.

As with most innovations, there is competitive confusion about names. The Post Office tried to register the name viewdata for its service, but this was refused on the ground that it was too all-embracing a title. Then it chose Prestel, and began a campaign to get viewdata accepted internationally as the generic term for computerized public information systems. That campaign is not going well: the European tendency is to prefer video-tex.

To confuse things further, there is also teletext. That is the (fairly) firmly established label for the similar, though more restricted, broadcasting services. Those originated in Britain as well; the BBC was first with its Ceefax service and Independent TV followed with Oracle. Teletext uses spare scan lines on the screen to provide the pages of information, which are therefore limited to a few hundred.

An even more significant difference between teletext and viewdata is that teletext is one way only, while viewdata is interactive – that means the messages can flow both ways along the phone line, so that you can cross-question the central computers. There lies the key to the wide range of services that viewdata may eventually supply, services that could play havoc with many traditional professions and trades, destroying cosy business – and trade union – boundaries.

Take income tax as an example. The average innumerate citizen never thinks of employing a tax consultant. He or she struggles with the annual form with irritated inefficiency. Viewdata could provide a question-and-answer service which would virtually complete that form for the average employee or self-employed businessman, and make sure they didn't miss any allowances.

Take holidays and travel. You would not need to go to a travel agent or wait eternally on the phone for rail or air enquiry offices to condescend to answer. You could book trains, flights, hotel rooms, excursions (and pay for them directly by credit-card code) from your home TV.

Take the infant chip-germinated industry of computer games. Viewdata already covers much of the range and could eventually add the dimension of playing chess with a friend in Honolulu.

Take classified advertising. Viewdata could save you the bother of hunting through the columns. You could tell the computer to put on your screen all houses available not more than twenty miles but not less than fifteen from, say, Edinburgh city centre, costing between £30,000 and £35,000, with a garden of at least half an acre, and with ... The list the computer would supply could be culled from half a dozen estate agents.

Take newspapers in general. No longer need they be centrally printed, carted round the country, and finally delivered to your home when their news is five to ten hours late. The British Post Office expects viewdata to be offering instant home printouts of newspapers (with, of course, full-colour pictures) by the early 1990s. That may be a conservative estimate: an English-language daily in Tokyo began experimenting with electronic facsimile delivery of its editions to hotels and businesses in 1978.

Take the mail order business. You could compare all the offerings on viewdata, then press a key to buy the goods you want. (In September 1979, a London wine club made claim to that minor bit of history: the first direct sales via the home TV screen, on the Prestel viewdata service. The security of the deal over those cases of wine is provided by the computer adding to the credit-card number the name and address of the Prestel TV receiver from which the order came. The wine is sent only to that address. The attempted fiddles have begun as well: the wine club says that some would-be customers have tapped out some 'very peculiar' credit-card numbers; it assumes charitably that they were 'practising' to get used to the system.)

And take the mail itself. Many big businesses have moved into electronic mail on company networks; viewdata could provide the first national electronic mail and message service, supplying the final death blow to the post, restricting the hobby of philately to history, and pulling even stamp dealers into the whirlpool of change.

Those examples skim the surface of viewdata's potential. Here are some random dips into the variety of information already being sold on the Prestel system: a guide to every establishment in Kensington High Street, London (that slightly baffling one is by courtesy of the magazine *Time Out*); tables for chocolate-bar salesmen so that they can check their firm's regional stocks before they leave home for the road; likewise, a list from an engineering firm of parts in stock, down to pages of countersunk head screws; cattle prices in Welsh; and a Bible Society selection of texts to call upon if you are tense or angry – or happy. Most of the pages are, of course, more down to earth: share prices, stockbrokers' analysts' reports, rail and air timetables, sports results, theatre reviews, job vacancies, advice services, and restaurant and car-buying guides.

Thus we can see that just one use of the silicon chip, already commercially available, holds in itself alone the potential to change society within a few years. And if we try to look further ahead – but still restricting ourselves essentially to the viewdata concept – we can see the line to changes much more profound.

Politics, for instance. If every home had a viewdata TV set, then democracy could – if we wanted – become literally government by the people, and instant government at that, with daily push-button voting even on secondary issues. One of the most blissful assumptions made about Jane Babbage's world in Chapter 2 was that we could muster the maturity to make that work. In some US cities, where cable TV links most of the homes, immediate electronic polling has been used to test voters' views on local government issues. The implications of this were bravely faced by the British government's think tank, the Central Policy Review Staff, in a report to the Cabinet in 1978: 'Any interactive television system, such as Prestel, provides a potential channel for a poll which is immediate, cheap, and increasingly universal ... The potential influence on the processes of both central and local government is substantial.'

An issue that could become almost equally controversial is the effect of viewdata on professions like medicine and the law, and the layman's reliance on them. There is a computer technique which a group of UK computer scientists have labelled 'knowledge refining'. It enables the best specialists to distil their knowledge and experience for the use of lesser medical mortals. Joe Babbage was putting it into practice in Chapter 2. Some American hospitals have been experimenting with it since the late 1970s, with interns turning to the computer for advice after examining patients.

The computer gains its knowledge through a series of cross-questioning sessions with the human expert. This is said to produce a big improvement in codified knowledge, particularly in what mathematicians might call the messy areas, like medicine. Chess makes a good analogy; in fact, it has been used as a test-bed. The chess master feeds the computer with all the bits of advice he can recall about tackling a particular problem. The computer analyses these 'rules' and, in dialogue with the master, considers many different sequences of events. This process produces a code of advice both simpler and more consistent than the expert's original. Professor Donald Michie, head of the machine intelligence unit at Edinburgh University, has put the 'unifying principle' in this way: 'A reliability and competence of codification can be produced which far surpasses the highest level that the unaided human expert has ever, and perhaps even could ever, attain.'

Put that sort of thing on viewdata, and the home medical guide and everyman's lawyer become a totally different – and more dangerous? – kettle of fish. Yet it is only one stage beyond the sort of question-the-computer advice services already contemplated.

The more immediate implications of viewdata are controversial enough. The service is today colliding with laws enacted long before such a technology was possible. The issues being negotiated, as the bureaucracy and the pressure groups awaken to what the new medium means, include copyright, obscenity, libel, privacy, advertising codes, editorial controls, consumer protection – even Value Added Tax.

The VAT problem, at least, is comedy. Customs and Excise officials decided that VAT should be charged on the information carried by Prestel, though VAT is not charged on newspapers, magazines and books. The reasoning was that the VAT exemption regulations (drawn up in ancient days – 1973) mentioned printed publications but said nothing about electronic screens. The association formed by companies providing information on Prestel argued in vain that there is no difference in principle between information provided on paper and information sold on the TV screen. In any case, the information can be transferred from screen to paper, via a printer. The issue was about to go to a VAT tribunal when Treasury ministers intervened to restore common sense and to decree viewdata VAT-free.

Such problems of adjustment are complicated by the fact that the Post Office is acting solely as the middle man, the carrier of information between the organizations contributing to the service and the people receiving it; and the Post Office is accepting no responsibility for what it regards as censorship. Another complication is that the information-suppliers can alter that information quickly and continually through their own editing terminals linked to the Post Office computers. That is, of course, a crucial requirement for services like stock market prices and sports results. But, in other areas, it could open the door to a slow-motion version of subliminal advertising – wild claims or vicious libels slotted in for two minutes a day.

The Post Office reply to that indicates one of the many differences between the electronic media and their print-bound predecessors: it would be virtually impossible – even if it were right in principle – to keep a continual check on thousands, then millions, of pages, many of which are being altered many times a day.

One basic issue is how to define the distinction between impartial information and advertising. The UK's Advertising Standards Authority and the Prestel information suppliers took nearly a year to agree on a draft code of practice applicable to the extra dimension of viewdata. The British Medical Association is also worried about 'misleading information' and is fond of quoting the 'quite frightening' possibility of an advertisement getting in for 'Mr Smith's potion which will cure anything from cancer to rheumatism'.

But Alex Reid, the young director of Prestel (young, that is, in Post Office language : he's in his late thirties), is belligerent in his opposition to what he sees as censorship. 'We feel', he says, 'that the imposition of any non-statutory limitations is the beginning of a slippery slope.' He is particularly irate about attempts to vet medical material – 'a very subjective' area – and he would resent 'very strongly indeed' any attempts at vetting by the Medical Association. In discussing the problem, he recalls with a grin that in one of his first meetings with the Advertising Standards Authority the question of advertising herbal remedies was raised – 'as a crunch argument that would break my nerve.'

The Post Office's one concession is to offer home censorship. If, for instance, a customer objects to his children obtaining contraceptive advice, he will be able to block out that part of the system. Prestel's first censorship challenge occurred in 1980 – because one information-providing firm offered a light-hearted guide to the porn shops of Soho.

Reid also rejects the Big Brother fears about viewdata. He argues that there are fewer totalitarian dangers than there are with TV, radio or newspapers. With the Post Office acting solely as the carrier of other people's information, variety of sources is assured.

So much for the social challenges. The business challenges equally illustrate the complexities of change. Viewdata looks a sure bet in the long run, an inevitable component of informatics, as the computer screen replaces the phone as a more dexterous centre of communication in office and home. But, in the short-term, it is a high-risk enterprise.

Britain has a two-year lead but that lead is narrowing. Many other nations are hustling to produce similar national systems. The emergence of Prestel was delayed, first by computer problems at the Post Office, then by the slowness of the British television manufacturers in getting into mass production with the adapted TV sets on which the service

depends. Part of the problem, technically, was the fundamental decision to put all the necessary microelectronics
within the set itself, rather than produce a black box which
might have sold, for attachment to existing sets, at less than
£100. The earliest Prestel receivers cost nearly £1000.

Prestel exhibits all the problems of getting in first:
initial technical troubles, then the need to build a mass
market quickly so that costs can fall. What's more, the solid
evidence of an immediate domestic market is scanty: the
more primitive, broadcast teletext services have been operating since 1974 without exciting wide public interest – and
their information comes free. (There were, at most, 45,000
teletext receivers in use in Britain at the end of 1979.)

Prestel customers are being charged by the Post Office at
local phone call rates, plus three pence a minute during
business hours and three pence for three minutes at other
times. The firms supplying the information can also charge
the customer, and those charges can vary from a half penny
to ten pence per screenful – and up to fifty pence for pages
of highly specialized business data.

In all, it could cost twenty pence just to find out the
latest share prices or the winner of the 2.30 at Newmarket.
(The central computers automatically debit the customer;
each page for which there is a charge shows that charge, and
the screen also tells you how much you have spent in total
on each use of the system.)

It seems, therefore, that much of the early market will be
in business use – particularly through cheaper, smaller,
monochrome desktop receivers. Several major companies
have established internal viewdata networks to carry company information and to link into the public service; multinational electronic groups, like Philips and GEC, are selling
company viewdata systems; and there are several combina-
tions of smaller businesses, such as travel agents and
booksellers, setting up national but private networks to
supply trade information and electronic transactions for

their members (these already have their jargon designation: closed-user groups).

Internationally, there is a variety of approaches to the technicalities of presenting viewdata and this has led to the usual, frustrating, nationalistic squabbles about setting an international standard so that viewdata networks can interlock world-wide. The last vestiges of the *entente cordiale* in telecommunications vanished when the British Post Office virtually accused the French of sabotaging a Prestel demonstration in Paris.

France, in fact, has taken the most imaginative route: the government is planning to supply free viewdata sets to every phone user. There is an economic rationale to this, as well as the strategic element of spreading computer-awareness. France is behind West Germany and Britain in phone usage and there is a drive to increase the number of phones installed by 200,000 a year throughout the 1980s. That presents a progressive problem in publishing phone directories – they are always about one third out of date. So France has decided to scrap phone books entirely and to leave directory enquiries to a computer system, somewhat like the British CAFS system described in Chapter 5, but with the customers communicating directly with the computer. They are using simple computer terminals for the purpose and they estimate that, in mass production, these could cost less than £50 each. Therefore, it should prove cheaper to give these away rather than continually update and reprint the phone books. And the French viewdata service, on trial in 1981, is included in the package, though only in a black-and-white version.

The most sophisticated use of colour so far is in the Bell-Canada version of video-tex, which can handle photographs and maps, but the photographs take several seconds to build up on the screen. Prestel's current graphics are less convincing, because they have to be constructed from tiny squares – no curves. In Canada and France it is intended to use video-tex for the sort of home services contemplated in the Japanese blueprint of a decade before – electricity meter reading, burglar alarms and fire detection.

The United States has several localized services, ranging from the Prestel one, being sold there for business use, to small electronic newspapers serving home computers in California. Japan and Sweden are running trials and Britain has sold Prestel to Germany, Holland and Hong Kong.

For Europe, where telecommunications are run by national authorities, the viewdata concept seems to have arrived in the nick of time: just when those authorities needed to adjust to a more central role in their nations' economies, as communications become increasingly important. They, more than most, need to abandon fixed career patterns in response to the demands of friskier, short-lived technologies.

The UK's Prestel team reflects this. Reid is a former naval helicopter pilot who went into telecommunications from architecture and urban planning. Some of his key people are even more remote from the Post Office photofit. For example, there is Ederyn Williams, a thirty-three-year-old psychologist, shoulder-length-haired and natty-suited, who has been recruited to find ways to increase the effectiveness of viewdata for the average user.

The Post Office is encouraging the middle man in view-data design and Williams's work therefore connects closely with the growing industry of viewdata services. He advocates the adaptation of the classic rules of typography to the narrow window of the TV screen and is caustic about the 'paintbox syndrome' of ill-judged clusters of colours, over-elaborate graphics and flashing symbols. Here he bites the hand that feeds him by citing one of the Post Office's own frames – a highly-coloured, winking, left-wing-flapping version of the Post Office's advertising symbol, bird Buzby.

The bulk of the growing viewdata service industry is devoted to what the Post Office calls the 'umbrella information-provider'. These are companies that act as brokers or wholesalers for Prestel pages, taking under their umbrella firms that want to put information on Prestel but lack computer expertise and/or knowledge of the new medium. Most of the umbrellas are off-shoots of established consultancies, computer bureaux and software houses.

A few are looking to the longer-term logic of viewdata in the home and small business – devising methods that will enable viewdata to become a channel for sending program packages into home computers to instruct those computers in particular jobs. (Several Japanese companies are working on TV sets that will be computers in their own right – orchestrating viewdata, organizing TV recordings and music centres, and controlling the home's lighting, heating and cookers.)

Other service companies are looking for virgin territory for viewdata, trying to ensure that it does not merely mimic the older media of print and broadcasting. The pioneer here was Richard Hooper as managing director of Mills and Allen Communications. In 1980 he moved on to lead the Post Office Prestel team under Reid.

Hooper is fond of the analogy of the first railway carriages that looked like horse-drawn coaches. One idea Mills and Allen have produced in their efforts to avoid that trap is a fund-raising one. The Save the Children Fund have taken Prestel pages to ask people to give ten pence to help a child in, say, Pakistan. If the customer presses the appropriate key to say yes, his account is debited ten pence and a page comes on to the screen telling the story of the child concerned. Another idea is for organizations under attack to put their case direct to the public. Hooper believes that the treatment of news could be altered by viewdata, because the different parties to a dispute could 'state their views without them necessarily being edited and woven into a narrative by an intermediary.'

Inventing new uses for viewdata has become a standard game of computer people – paralleling the game of challenging sceptics to name a task that the microprocessor could not perform. Yet it is arguable that viewdata is not strictly an invention at all.

The idea came from a man nearing retirement, Sam Fedida. After RAF wartime work on radar, Fedida spent twenty years on the research side of the Marconi company. He was fifty-two when he joined the Post Office to head a new research division. His brief was to stimulate new ideas in using computers and, within a few months, he had persuaded the Post Office that the road to take was a computerized information service, simple to operate, and employing proven technology – though, at that time, much of the enthusiastic talk was about view-phones (which are also just beginning). Apparently, the Post Office hierarchy did not then appreciate the implications; they became enamoured of the idea on the basis that it would boost off-peak phone calls. Fedida's viewdata was ready for demonstration in 1974, but it did not become publicly available until 1979.

Some detractors say that viewdata is just an inevitable progression, an orthodox computer network broadened to public and national size. Others point out that the idea really began in the United States in the early 1960s with a succession of reports from academic think tanks. But what Fedida did do was to see the logic of linking the phone to the TV set – and to the publishing industry.

Those US reports – Martin Greenberger at the Massachusetts Institute of Technology in 1964, Douglas Parkhill at the Mitre Corporation in 1966, and Paul Baran's massive study of the future of the phone for AT&T in 1971 – provide another example of the way in which the futurologists' projections from the computer's infancy were dubiously dismissed as crying wolf. They mentioned most of the services that viewdata now offers, but their emphasis tended to be on yet another of the 'society' labels of which futurologists are so fond – the Cashless Society.

Just as the shrinking of the computer on to the chip is

at last making harsh, competitive, economic sense of those extravagant early forecasts of peopleless factories, so it is producing a profit motive for getting rid of money.

Let's pick up that adjoining piece of the jigsaw.

7. Getting rid of money

The combination of two rawly competitive industries – the retail trade and computer manufacturing – is building a structure that is changing the meaning of money. The futurologists' theory is that the silicon chip will make computer networks cheap enough to get rid of cash – and of the half-way houses of cheques and credit cards. All transactions will then be electronic, with bank accounts being automatically and instantly debited when a purchase is made, either at a computerized store checkout or a home computer terminal, à la viewdata.

But most bankers say that the Cashless Society will take a long time to develop and that cash may never completely disappear – its anonymity is too useful to the tax-dodging moonlighter and to the wife/husband who does not want the husband/wife to know where the money is going. The retail trade is also cautious about the speed of change, but less so than the banks. For instance, David Barrett, financial director of one of Britain's big supermarket chains, Fine Fare, points out that ninety-nine per cent of supermarket sales are still in cash. Therefore the department stores, with their greater proportion of credit-card customers, will lead the way. Nevertheless, he forecasts that the totally electronic transaction will be commonplace within ten to fifteen years.

The framework is certainly growing, with the US in the lead and the rest of the developed world catching up fast. One example of the complexity involved is a UK clothing chain with 360 branches: in 1980 all the computer-run tills in all those shops were joined in one national network that gives head office a daily check on the action, in total and in detail.

The reasoning behind the retail trade's automation is not the cashless sale: it is greater competitiveness. For the department-store chain, dealing with a wide range of goods, many of them subject to the whims of fashion, the immediate yet nationwide check is a boon; not simply so that stocks can be replenished quickly in this or that store, but also to guide buying policy. That's seductive for the supermarkets, too, but in their case the greater emphasis is on speed at the till – and, often, cutting the number of checkout staff.

Therefore, the supermarkets are the first to introduce the second stage of automation: the use of laser scanners, linked to the computers, to read fuller details of the purchase from a bar-coded label. The recording of each purchase – and the printing of the bill – can then take less than a second. All the checkout staff have to do is to pass the packet over a slot through which the laser beam reads the label.

The bar code could become as common a symbol of the computer's secondary effects on our daily lives as the pocket calculator. It is appearing on books as well as washing powder. It is a small printed pattern of black-on-white bars of varying thickness. Those differences in thickness, when read by the laser scanner, give the store computer a variety of information about the goods, including origin, description and price.

This makes it possible to change prices immediately (the computer has only to be told to interpret the bars differently) or to offer percentage reductions for big purchases. The customer gets the advantages of a more detailed receipt, less queueing at the checkouts, and the end of operator errors or fiddles. The drawback is that prices are no longer displayed on the goods themselves, only on the shelves. Some consumer groups in the US have also complained that a few supermarkets have increased prices suddenly at the tills without changing the prices on the shelves, so that the package costing 2·10 dollars when you put it in your basket costs 2·20 half a minute later at the till. The patterns of the bar codes are decided by national number banks, organized jointly by the stores and the makers of the goods, and joining up in an international system.

Experiments directly linking store computers to bank computers to provide the cashless sale are underway in the US, France and Sweden. Negotiations for a British pilot trial began in 1978 and continued into 1980, with the Retail Consortium and the banks entangled in arguments about who should pay for the still-expensive equipment. In the trials, store customers in the chosen towns have their bank cards read by the computerized tills. For added security, the customer keys into the computer a personal code number before the electronic signal goes to the bank to debit his account.

The security of transactions might be further strengthened in the future by computers checking signatures and voice patterns. Computers are available today to spot forgeries, some working on the pressures of the pen, some on shapes, and some simply on the unvarying points of contact with the paper. Others can identify the structure of the individual human voice and obey that voice only, even if the individual concerned has caught a heavy cold since last talking to the computer.

Thus a structure is being built, the ultimate logic of which is the rejection of cash – yet its economic imperatives are cash-bound. Perhaps the clearest examples of this are in West Germany, a country which has not taken to the credit card with anything like the alacrity of North America and Britain. About a dozen store groups there use laser scanning.

On the outskirts of Munich there is a huge cash-and-carry warehouse with thirty-five laser checkouts. It has no truck with credit cards and is even a bit grudging about the Eurocheque. The logic of automation there is throughput:

200,000 items are sold daily and each checkout assistant handles four to five tons of merchandise in the day. The innkeepers and corner-store owners and their children – and other less legitimate users of wholesale trade permits – carry the stuff away by the vanload, after spending two to three hours wandering along the miles of shelves where they can buy anything from wine to lawn-mowers.

That store, run by the BLV group, has replaced price tags with laser-read labels on ninety-seven per cent of its goods, thirty-three per cent with the full European bar code and the rest with simpler number-coded labels. Automation has led to a reduction of twenty per cent in the number of checkout staff in BLV's smaller supermarkets. The computerized tills are also used to record each employee's work rate. (There are no bonus payments, but customers often tip.)

German department stores are also cutting staff while increasing trade through the computer. At the Breuninger store in Stuttgart (which 'likes to compare with Harrods') there is a policy of no redundancies, but staff savings through 'natural wastage' are running at about fifteen per cent a year. The president of that store group – Willem Van Agtmael, a charismatic Dutchman who, at thirty-three, is running a company with 3000 employees and annual business of £125 million – says that point-of-sale automation does not interest them directly: 'We could collect the money in cigar boxes.' The motivation for using the computer there is the breadth and speed of the management information that it supplies – plus staff savings, of course.

For the department-store customer the computer can become a nuisance, not a boon. At Breuninger they have to go to an office on the edge of the sales floor for the computer to record their purchases via a magnetic label. Thirty per cent of the sales are by credit card – but credit cards issued by the store, a practice that is growing in other countries too.

Getting rid of money

On the surface evidence, one might expect the banks to be advocates of the Cashless Society: physical money pushes a mountain of paperwork at them. One of the British clearing banks has calculated that its branches in one region handle 300,000 documents a week and each of these documents is handled ten times in its lifespan: all – theoretically – needless work. But that work represents a huge capital and human investment.

Nevertheless, the inexorable logic of automation is being widely applied in the banks, particularly in international work. The SWIFT computer network now links fifty banks in fifteen countries. For the ordinary customer the obvious signs are the computer-produced bank statement (sometimes making a nonsense through inadequate programming or other human input error) and the spread of out-of-hours, cash-dispensing computers at the branches.

These, of course, can provide not only cash but account statements and cheque books; in some cases they accept cash deposits as well. They operate by insertion of a bank card for the computer to read, plus the entry of the customer's code number on a keyboard. They are slowly spreading beyond bank branches to office blocks, airports, department stores and the factory floor.

There is now, too, an extensive range of computer systems that can link the banks and the shops. These complete the average transaction in less than a minute – from feeding in all the details of the transaction and recognizing the customer's personal identification number, to printing the transaction in a passbook or on a receipt. There are versions for bank branches and for banking services at the store till. On the teller's side of the window is a small computer terminal; on the customer's side a keyboard on which he enters his code number. That security number is not known by the teller – his terminal shows only that the correct information has been entered.

The banks are cautious about uniting these pieces into a

greater whole. Two consultants with the UK's Inter-Bank Research Organization, Peter Hirsch and John Railton, said in a report in 1978 that many commentators about the future of banking were taking a 'wholly unrealistic view' of the rate of change. Their research showed that about sixty per cent of the British clearing banks' staff were still involved in money transaction work. This represented a commitment of more than 100,000 employees, capital resources approaching £1 billion, and annual operating costs of about £800 millions.

Although the numbers of non-cash transactions, and the proportion of people paid by cheque, had increased steadily in the 1970s, they found no evidence of any significant reduction in the volume of cash transactions. They concluded that the distribution and collection of cash through the bank branches would remain a substantial element of the branch workload, 'even if drastic changes occur in the nature of bank branches or bank systems.' The dominance of cash was true for all the countries they examined. In the United States, for instance, the real value of cash in circulation continued to increase slowly year by year.

Hirsch and Railton pointed out that the clearing of inter-bank payments was more fully automated in Britain than in any other country, but they added: 'The picture of the money transfer market as a whole leads to the conclusion that ... radical change is likely to take place slowly. Far from the cashless and chequeless society becoming a reality in the near future, there seems to be little immediate prospect of an even less-cheque and less-cash society.'

Two years later, the banking world's general view seems less dogmatic than that. Bankers tend to say that – till the end of the century at least – the gradual emphasis will be on less cash and fewer cheques, the banks' motives being to reduce that paper work. The other factors pushing in that direction are formidable: the spread of plastic money (more than seven million people hold credit cards in the UK); the huge sums that the retail trade pays the banks for cash handling; and, tangentially, the advance of the automated office.

Automation of the office – then, maybe, the death of the office – is, logically, the next piece to slot into the jigsaw. But so far we have neglected one of the corner pieces: how is all this information shunted around the world? That collection of technologies also has its 'society' cliché – the Wired Society.

8. Of satellites and laser light

On 12 April 1979, the Australian Broadcasting Commission took an eccentric decision. It opened its mid-evening television news with an extravagant welcome to just another stage in space satellite communications – the confirmation of a stronger link to the other side of the world with the official opening of a satellite earth station in the English countryside at Madley, near Hereford. The penultimate scenes of Uganda's release from Idi Amin took second place to an exchange of pictures and platitudes between Australia and Britain, via a contraption weighing less than 500 pounds and poised 22,300 miles above the Indian Ocean.

That Australian broadcast painted a shrewd lesson about one of the major developments of the 1970s that we have quickly come to accept for granted : immediate and high-quality global communication via satellite. In the mid-1960s there were only half a dozen civilian satellite earth stations training their massive eyes at the sky. Now there are more than 200, bouncing their radio signals on nearly twenty orbiting electronic mirrors. Those numbers are being raised rapidly in the 1980s.

International satellite communications are provided by Intelsat, a 101-nation organization in which the United States (twenty-five per cent) and Britain (eleven per cent) are the biggest partners. Intelsat was running thirteen satellites at the start of the 1980s, six dealing with trans-Atlantic traffic, four over the Indian Ocean and three over the Pacific. In addition, there are the domestic satellites, a status symbol born in the US and, so far, adopted by

France and India; a European set of communications satellites is due to begin operation in 1981; and then there are, of course, the military, maritime and weather satellites.

Although transocean cables are also being extended and modernized, satellites now handle about seventy per cent of international phone calls. The number of calls is doubling every four to five years and the transmission of computer data and TV broadcasts is multiplying even faster. The spread of satellite communications contains the same lesson as the spread of the silicon chip: costs are cut both by the technology itself and by the increased use of it. For instance, international trunk dialling from Britain (now available to nearly ninety countries, with use increasing by twenty-five per cent a year) means that a three-minute call to Australia costs £3.15. In 1930, when the phone service to Australia began, three minutes cost £6 – equivalent to about £86 at 1980 prices.

But the increase in satellite traffic is still not matching demand. A dialled call to the United States from London in the rush-hour of English afternoon/American morning is an odds-against gamble with the recorded voice: 'All international lines are engaged – please try later.'

The dish aerial opened at Madley in 1979 (it has a diameter of 105 feet and cost £6 millions) is to be joined by five more in the 1980s. And in the contrastingly arid landscape of Goonhilly Downs in Cornwall, where Britain's first satellite earth station was opened in 1962, the current total of four dish aerials is due to be doubled. The British Post Office is spending £1 billion a year in its attempts to keep pace.

The needs of expansion are being met not only by new satellites and earth stations but by richer use of them. The fourth Goonhilly disc, 62 feet in diameter, and the European Space Agency's test satellite OTS 2, have been teamed to test three main methods of packing in more work in the transition from the old wave form of sending speech to the computerized form of digital signals. These are: each earth station using the same satellite radio channel in sequence in a series of synchronized bursts of transmission; interspersing the impulses of one phone conversation in the pauses that occur in other conversations; and transmitting two groups of phone calls together from one aerial – one horizontally polarized, the other vertically polarized (one of the problems being investigated there is how much atmospheric conditions affect the degree of isolation between those two beams).

Progress since the pioneer days has been considerable. The first Madley aerial can carry over 2000 phone calls at once, more than twice the capacity of the first Goonhilly aerial, which carried the Indian Ocean satellite calls, serving forty countries, before Madley took over. As for the satellites themselves, the latest Atlantic Ocean ones handle 12,000 calls at a time.

All these satellites are in geo-synchronous orbit. That is, they move at the same speed as the rotation of the earth, so they stay over their destined part of the globe, on the equator, 22,300 miles up. They have jet motors, run by compressed air, to keep them from wandering. And it's a neat coincidence that the store of compressed air lasts about as long as the usefulness of the ageing satellite – three to four years. The satellites get the energy they need from sunlight.

The US is well into the second stage of satellite use: much smaller dish aerials providing communication to an office from the rooftop or even a window ledge. The third stage – the personal aerial in the garden – is being advertised in the American Christmas gift catalogues. The main advantage of that, so far, is to have a wider variety of TV films at your disposal, but this piece of one-upmanship for the rich raises an issue we have not faced so far – the coming impact of global communication on the have-nots.

I had my first lesson on this subject back in 1976. The

editor of a major Indian newspaper was looking from his office balcony at the rush-hour below. Overloaded buses and battered cars jousted with tricycle taxis, and the pavements were an even tighter tangle of humanity. 'India should ban the transistor radio,' he said. That bitter reaction to the migration from the villages to the city slums is echoed today in less likely quarters.

James Martin is the up-market guru of computer communications. Formerly in the upper reaches of IBM, he now conducts mass seminars around the world. In his book *The Wired Society*, he points out that many of the new uses of telecommunications are in conflict with the established order and will encounter fierce opposition from vested interests; but he also concedes that the benefits could accrue on the basis of the rich getting richer, widening the margin of envy.

Martin says the expansion of satellite communications will hammer the people of the developing nations with the most cunningly persuasive advertisements, 'because this is how multinational corporations will maximize their profits.' He fears the sort of currents that could be generated when 'the world's billions are wired together' and expresses little hope of international cooperation or even of politicians and administrators learning how to assess the advances in telecommunications.

The business use of commercial satellites is another example of the convergence between computing and telecommunications. IBM is the power behind Satellite Business Systems, the American consortium that hopes to challenge the traditional US telecommunication operators, like Western Union and AT&T, in satellites. It is promising a service that will include video-phone conferences and a deluxe version of electronic mail, transmitting letters at a rate of 3600 pages an hour.

Video phones and the electronic transmission of documents are oldish technologies: Britain has had a little-used video-phone service since 1971 and the facsimile trans-mission of documents (docfax in the Newspeak jargon) goes back twenty-five years. It's another case of microelectronics meeting the expansion in the demand for communications with a service both cheaper and smarter.

The British Confravision service, based on stations in London, Bristol, Birmingham, Manchester and Glasgow, is still only being used to ten per cent of capacity. Mobile stations are being introduced to overcome the obvious problem, but the main snag is that it still costs £60 for thirty minutes. Europe's first Confravision link by satellite was organized by the British Post Office at an international telecommunications exhibition in Geneva in 1979. Visitors to the exhibition were able to cross-question a Confravision team in London and see themselves and the London trio on adjoining screens at the same time. TV pictures and sound from the conference studio went by cable to a dish aerial in a car-park nearby. From there they were beamed to the European test satellite and bounced down to Goonhilly. The signals finally travelled from Cornwall to London by microwave link. All that takes about a second.

The spread of such view-phones to the likes of you and me is hardly likely in the 1980s, but docfax is definitely gaining its second, microelectronic wind. Here again we meet the central principle of changing methods of com-munication from the analog wave form to the digital.

In the early days, the uses of docfax were largely re-stricted to newspapers, law offices and the few other busi-nesses that dealt in lots of documents that people far away needed to see quickly – comparatively quickly, that is, for the facsimile copy of the average letter on an A4 sheet could take two to three minutes to build up on the receiving machine from the electronic messages sent down the phone line. Now that those messages are chopped up into nought-and-one bits, the letter can be there in half a minute.

Part of the increase in speed comes from a simple computer gimmick called data compression: the scanner that 'reads' the page is told to ignore the white space and record only the black letters and, since so little of the space on a letter contains the actual message, this shrinking of the transmission – it's spaced out again at the receiving end – saves a lot of time.

If you boost that with microelectronics, laser-beam scanning and fast non-impact methods of printing, you cut the time again. The American company AM International has combined these techniques to make a prototype system which it claims is about 120 times faster than the old analog facsimile transmission machines – and produces a better copy, 'comparing favourably' with the original document.

Thus we should see letters delivered to the other side of the world within seconds by the mid-1980s. But high-speed facsimile equipment is still too expensive for the little business. An answer now being applied is the electronic-mail sorting office, offering its services to the public. Computers store the letters and transmit all the mail for a particular city in one burst over the satellite. The receiving mail offices then reproduce the documents and distribute them. An international service on these lines has begun between New York and London.

Plans are also being made to combine that use of satellites with the quick-search capabilities of the specialized information banks (discussed in Chapter 5). The British Library is looking at the possibility of using docfax to supply microfilmed versions of the papers held in its databank. Thereby a technical manager in Tokyo or a scientist in Sydney, knowing vaguely of a research paper he should consult, could trace that paper on his computer terminal and have the paper delivered to his desk, all within a minute. But why then bother to use docfax at all when he could read the abstract on his screen and get a hard copy from his computer printer?

That is one of the many fascinating unsolved equations raised by the pace at which each new development is overtaken by the next. Is the current surge in the use of docfax just a temporary aberration before word-processors talking to word-processors becomes the norm and letters are transmitted straight from the computer keyboard? The answer will probably be decided by a balancing of cost, speed and convenience – with, maybe, a nice legal debate about the validity of electronically transmitted signatures.

In any event, satellites alone cannot cope with the expansion in telecommunications, particularly at local level. The answer here, till something better turns up, is the use of optical fibres, where pulses of light, travelling along minute glass tubes, replace electric cables.

Microelectronics weave their way into all we have discussed in this chapter, and fibre-optics are equally in the world of the microscopic. Light signals beat electricity on most counts: greater capacity, wider versatility, firmer accuracy (there's no electro-magnetic noise to corrupt a message), easier to install, and becoming cheaper. Fibre-optic cables began to take over the phone networks of North America, Western Europe and Japan at the start of the 1980s.

The advance they represent can be shown on a scale of three. At the bottom is the ordinary electric phone cable, which still carries the bulk of traffic, both ordinary speech and the digital talk between computer and computer. A cable holding 4800 pairs of wires – one wire, one conversation – is arm-thick. Its successor electrically – the co-axial cable – needs only eighteen sets of more complex wires occupying slightly more than half the space, because it uses advanced electronics at its ends to sort out the messages. Co-axial cables provide the cable television that serves about 15 million American homes. Most can carry forty TV channels but, in theory, they could carry hundreds.

The equivalent fibre-optic cable is thinner than a finger

and needs only eight tubes to do the work of those original 4800 pairs of wires. The tubes are about a tenth of a milli-metre wide, so we are back with the cliché comparison of passing through the eye of a needle; and each tube carries eight million bits of information a second. The glass in the core of those tubes is of such pure transparency that a half-mile thick window of them would be as easy to see through as a pane of ordinary glass. There are fibres in the research labs that will allow ten per cent of light through for thirty miles. (And remember that the average window pane be-comes almost opaque after an inch or two if you try to look through it edge-on.)

Fibre-optic transmission is digital. The electrical pulses, representing the noughts and ones, are changed by a laser into the light pulses that travel along the tube. A single phone conversation would appear as a stream of 64,000 bits per second, but these conversations can be combined (the jargon word is 'multiplexing') so that 120 conversations are transmitted as eight million bits a second along one fibre.

Fibre-optics have another advantage. Co-axial cables re-quire repeaters about every mile, otherwise the electrical signals become distorted. For fibre-optic cables, those re-peaters can be six miles apart, and there are systems being developed that would allow them to be sixty miles apart. That simplicity and increased efficiency holds the usual employment implications: fewer men required to tinker down the manholes in the city pavements.

If we now lift our heads from the detail for a moment and put the elements together, we can see that the communica-tion requirements of a Jane Babbage world already exist: cables that can bring a multiplicity of services into the home and the satellite capability to make those links global. The evidence is also available for the jazzier details – the possi-bility of talking to Turin while walking down Fifth Avenue or holding a conference via a TV screen that hangs flat on the wall. But that evidence will be clearer if we first establish the basis on which this plethora of communication can be marshalled locally.

The answer, once more, is microelectronic – using the chip to convert phone exchanges, both on the public network and in the office, from their electro-mechanical basis to digtital, computer form. This process was well underway in the 1970s. In office terms, this means that the internal phone exchange becomes a computer, not only organizing the full range of office communications, data transmissions as well as voice, but also monitoring the whole process. The office manager can have a daily check on the phone bill – and know that Joe Bloggs used an office phone to call his girlfriend on holiday in Majorca and they talked for three-and-a-half minutes. In national terms, the phone network can become a single digital system, carrying voice, picture and computer communications.

Computerized exchanges offer the ability to bounce phone calls about like pinballs – transferring calls automatically from one extension to another; allowing you to speak to several people simultaneously, or add them one by one; and enabling an extension number to be altered instantly within the computer without having to change the wiring to the receiver. Until now, those things have tended to be confined to the big companies, but cheaper microelectronics are bringing them down the scale.

One example comes from Norway. The Ring company there has produced an internal exchange run by one micro-computer, which is contained in a suitcase-sized cabinet, which hangs on the office wall. It provides all the usual gimmicks, serves ninety-six extensions, and adds contact with radio-pagers and computer systems through touch-dialling. The handset is a twelve-button keypad. When placed on the desk, it acts as a loudspeaker phone; when you lift it to your ear, the volume drops. It also has individual volume control – and, above all, a switch to cut off incoming calls and leave you in peace.

Most digital phone exchanges are founded on formal computers, but another method of organizing huge flows of information is gaining increasing attention. It is akin to the distributed processing we discussed in Chapter 5. Its implications are much wider than the phone exchange, but that kind of use provides the best example so far.

The fundamental idea is that the arrival of the microprocessor means that you no longer have to think of a heavyweight computer as one machine. It can be a circle (a ring main) or a series of data highways, consisting of a vast army of chips which juggle the work around between them to provide both depth and speed of processing power. It could be likened to an anthill, but an anthill with more than a common intelligence, where each worker ant is far from dumb. It's a system without central processor or memory.

The Delphi Corporation, an off-shoot of the Exxon company, has such a system working in San Francisco. It is called Delta and it runs a phone-answering service. It has a double 'road', containing thirty-two processors, and each of those processors contains 800 silicon chips, giving each one power that rivals the big mainframe computers of a few years ago. So there are thirty-two computers in one. Those processors front much bigger memory storage.

Jay Stoffer, vice-president of Delphi, describes Delta as a 'self-healing community', because it monitors and remedies its own faults; if you yank out one circuit board, the system instantly switches the work to another battalion of the ant army. Delta can handle 250 million instructions a second, and it has been working around the clock since 1977. It could send and receive from a space satellite at a rate of sixty million bits a second – both ways. That speed is helped by another important technique of bulk communication: packet-switching.

The packet-switching method is to put the data into separate bundles for transmission, each bundle carrying a signal at its head giving the packet's destination. The bundles are unpacked at the receiving end and put together to provide the message. Packet-switching is used on Euronet, the European network that began to join up the Continent's information banks in 1980.

This transformation of telecommunications has clearly, if quietly, begun to change the way we live and work. It also has two important sectional effects : it promotes what we in Britain weirdly still call the Post Office to a more central role in the national economy, and, for the telecommunications equipment industry, it means revived business – but fewer jobs. The lesson of the new methods of manufacture – and the consequent simplifying of maintenance – can be condensed into one statistic : one silicon chip in the new generation of faster teleprinters replaces 900 parts that had to be assembled in the old electro-mechanical machines.

Britain has (at the time of writing) only one computerized local telephone exchange on the public network. It serves ninety customers around the village of Glenkindie, thirty miles west of Aberdeen. Throughout the second half of the 1970s the Post Office faced a bombardment of criticism, from government bodies as well as commercial interests, about its failure to match the demands made upon it to become a spearhead of change. Much of this criticism has centred on the slow development of System X, the computerized exchange system that is due to modernize the national phone network during the 1980s.

The signs of a new attitude are beginning to glimmer – in the plan to accept, after four years, a government inquiry's recommendation to make telecommunications a separate entity, in a less pernickety stance about competition, and in a slight shift of power from the civil-service mentality to an alliance of younger scientists and market-orientated frontmen. But enough of parochial concerns. The smaller elements leading towards the Jane Babbage world are also growing around us today. Let's begin with television.

The flat TV set to hang on the wall relies on a branch of microelectronics – opto-electronics – that is moving nearly as fast as the silicon chip itself. Its first everyday manifestation was in the displays on pocket calculators, using liquid crystals or light-emitting diodes. Most television manufacturers are now developing these methods to replace the bulky, bottle-like cathode ray tubes of the TV set. The Japanese companies Sanyo and Hitachi were among the first to produce experimental sets capable of mass production, early in 1978. Both have said they will have small, black-and-white sets on the market by 1981. The Sanyo version is only six millimetres thick.

It is easy to see that developing into large-screen versions, with clarity improved by perhaps thirty-five million individual points of light, produced by solid-state electronics. Large-screen TV is already available, anyway, through the less satisfactory projection methods.

Editing your own recordings of TV programmes, as the Babbages did, is also a current possibility in theory, though the equipment costs nearly £100,000 today. Once again we hit the basic principle: translate the TV signal into digits and you can play around with it instantly and endlessly – dividing the screen into quarters to provide four versions of the same event, slotting a window into the overall scene to magnify a detail of the action, or pulling a corner of the picture into full-screen close-up. TV channels have been using digital systems since 1977 to provide instant editing of live news and sports coverage. If you live in Britain you might not know that. The BBC and ITV finally accepted the idea late in 1979 – although a small British company, Quantel, was exporting digital editing systems to the United States and Japan in 1977.

Another aspect of the effect of microelectronics on broadcasting is the compact electronic news-gathering camera, which enables one man with an educated shoulder to replace a film crew – and which, more importantly, gets the information to the home customer at once.

The speed at which TV networks are converted from an analog to a digital basis is tied more to past investment in expensive analog equipment than to technical considerations. An important advantage of digital TV is in recordings. Analog video tape degenerates every time it is copied, thus restricting the amount of editing that is possible. Engineers at the UK Independent Broadcasting Authority say that about five generations of tape is the limit, whereas their digital version can produce at least twenty without loss of quality.

Television, however, is on the periphery of the collection of factors which is starting to push Western society towards home work. More important is the alliance between the automation of factory and office and the advance of the home computer and the portable computer terminal.

The progress of the personal computer has been impressive, first in the United States, then in Europe. The first models went on full sale in Britain early in 1978: twenty months later there were about 40,000 in use, in schools, offices, laboratories, homes, and the spreading computer clubs. That 40,000 estimate is for glossily cabineted microcomputers sold from the store shelves. Thousands more have been built from kits by computer buffs.

Their prices range from £100 (for a book-sized machine without its own display screen) up to £10,000 for the sort of full system serving the small business. Many are sold in specialist computer shops, though the swift growth of those shops received a check at the opening of the 1980s from the competition of the big retail groups. Those computer shops bridge the generation gap. The book and magazine browsers and keyboard-tappers include the schoolboy, the student, the businessman and the retired engineer. But, rather more than in the formal computer business, it's a mainly male and young world.

The personal computer is, of course, a direct product of

the microprocessor. A typical machine is little bigger than a typewriter, with a small television screen above the keyboard, as in the usual computer terminal or word-processor. A small printer can be attached, and plug-in cassettes or magnetic discs are used to store permanent data and the various programs.

The salesman's dream of these computers being used by the housewife – to learn languages at home or work out the family budget in graphs and diagrams on the screen, run the central heating and the cooker, or store phone numbers and recipes – has yet to materialize. The biggest single sale categories so far are small businesses and schools – people who could not afford the offerings of the mainstream computer manufacturers. The microcomputer covers most of the requirements of the little business – if enough money is spent on the software.

Their weirder uses include employment by an astrologer to produce birth charts; by a bookmaker to calculate how much money to lay off immediately before a race (that bookmaker has now formed a company to sell his system to other bookmakers); and by a fence (a police raid found him using a personal computer – legally bought – to keep check of his stock).

The number of different microcomputers on sale in Western Europe increased through 1979 at a rate of about two models per month to a total of more than sixty. Almost all of those were American, though Japan, inevitably, became a competitor by 1980. An extensive service industry is also developing – consultancies, software houses and maintenance companies running in parallel to the world of traditional computing. Among them are a few unscrupulous 'experts' and shady dealers. To combat that minority, UK dealers have formed a Computer Retailer Association with a strict code of conduct.

The next stage is the pocket computer. To define when this has arrived is mainly a problem in semantics. Just as it is difficult to distinguish the difference between an up-market microcomputer and a down-market minicomputer, so it is difficult to say when hand-held terminals exchanging information with parent computers down the phone line (or, for that matter, the latest programmable pocket calculators) become computers in their own right.

Semantics apart, it is clear that all the elements that allowed Jane Babbage to do much of her work while walking along the beach are available today. The wandering phone and the miniature TV are here, and the portable computer terminal, communicating by radio or phone line, is in widespread use. The research laboratories are putting those elements together in a tighter package, which may be up and running by the time you read this: Jane Babbage's pocket computer-communicator could look like the cordless phones on sale today. At the top would be a small extending aerial, and in the hand-cupped section between earpiece and mouthpiece, a miniature TV screen and a keyboard (though the latter should become superfluous as voice communication with computers progresses).

One problem of mass use would be to find space on the radio frequency spectrum, even in the ultra-high frequencies, but the research people of Motorola, the American microelectronics company whose pocket phone had successful street trials in Washington and Baltimore in 1979, say that the problem is solvable; already, they point out, the size of radio channel has been reduced four times.

The evidence for the other elements of the computer-communicator is also abundant, though TV-receivers will have to shrink a bit more before they slot into the phone. The smallest of the miniature TV sets so far has a two-inch screen, which provides surprising clarity of picture, but the set itself is just beyond pocket range. Its comparative bulk is caused by the fact that it uses a miniature version of the cathode-ray tube, not an opto-electronics display.

Inevitably, miniaturization has been galloping faster in

computers. One of the earliest versatile pocket terminals was developed in Sweden in 1977. It is the size of an antiquated pocket calculator, and it plugs into the phone line to communicate with a central computer. The original thought was that it would be used for order entry and stock control in warehouses, but it has since been used for collecting market research information, for production control in factories, and for meter reading. The original version had a memory capacity of 8000 characters but that has since been extended to 60,000.

The German Post Office has estimated that 50,000 radio computer terminals will be in use in West Germany by 1985. These are a bit bulkier than the phone-line ones, and are starting work at airports, docks and railway shunting yards in situations where a traffic controller, foreman or driver needs to be in fairly constant two-way communication with a central computer when he is away from phone points. One example, developed by the Geet company in Hamburg, is carried in a shoulder bag. It has a keyboard dealing in both words and numbers and the computer's replies are displayed on a small two-line screen.

Quite a number of the bright ideas in these areas come from small, new companies, providing support for the establishment faith that microelectronics creates new employment through entrepreneurial enterprise. One of the contributors to the growing selection of portable computers is a company called PBM, set up in 1979 (with their own money) by four British technologists and a former civil servant previously concerned with the government's microelectronics propaganda campaign. They are making a computer contained in a case twenty inches, by fourteen, by six-and-a-half, and weighing sixteen pounds. In that space, they say, they can provide the travelling businessman with sufficient processing power and storage to enable him to carry his records and accounts and process and update them along the way.

Their machine has a 480-character display screen (supplied by opto-electronics), disc storage, a typewriter-sized keyboard, and a phone-line connector that will join the user to viewdata services as well as a company's home computers. They are now working on a Mark II, made lighter and more compact by replacing the storage discs with bubble memories. Then they intend to add voice communication with the computer.

Bubble memories have been used in 'intelligent' computer terminals for some time. Texas Instruments sells a briefcase model which enables you to edit messages before dispatching them down the phone line. It is used by journalists to put reports straight into their newspapers' computers, and by salesmen to make orders and gather information from their headquarters' computers.

Not surprisingly, the computer industry itself leads the way in using this collection of opportunities to do more work from home. Many managers in computer companies have home terminals, and there are signs that computer-programming at home could be the biggest of the cottage industries of the 1980s. At least one British company – F International – works entirely that way.

In eighteen years, F International has grown from a one-woman company, started with £6 capital, to a group employing more than 600 freelance computer specialists. All those 600 – including the directors and the project managers – work at home on computer terminals, and most are women with young families. Of the non-specialist staff of a hundred, only twenty work in the token office, which is housed in the servants' wing of an eighteenth-century mansion at Chesham in Buckinghamshire.

Mrs Steve Shirley, the group's founder, stopped working at a big computer company when her baby son was born, and set up as Freelance Programmers. That was in 1962 – medieval times in computer count. Her aim was to cure the waste of talent among family-raising women computer specialists. But she is not a party-line feminist; the F in F International is for freelance, not female. She probably irritates orthodox libbers with her view that women's attention to detail makes them better computer programmers than men, while men are superior as systems and business analysts – 'very few women can do it,' she says.

Since the Sex Discrimination Act came into force the group has had to redirect its staff advertising to 'people with domestic responsibilities'. But this definition does not cover the field. Several of the freelance programmers are homebound by disablement, and one of the few men is an opera singer. He represents the romantic opportunities of this futuristic working pattern. Previously he had to earn his living entirely by programming and confine his singing to amateur societies. Now he can take professional jobs in the chorus and program while 'resting'.

Those who dismiss that sort of example as a pipedream rarity, with no significance for most of us, might not only be missing the meaning of the blend of current technologies described in this chapter: they could also be accused of ignoring the historical trends of shorter working hours and decreasing demand for semi-skilled work. The acceleration of that trend in the 1970s has been as clear in the office as in the factory. It is the job of the next chapter to demonstrate that.

9. Jobs that have gone

The effects of the pre-chip computer on the office, well within two decades, supplies the most telling evidence to support the orthodox argument that technological advance has always created new jobs to replace those destroyed. Banking and insurance could not have expanded at the rate they have without the computer, and where are all those wages clerks?

But, in trying to grasp the further acceleration of change that began in the late 1970s, it is useful to look at what went before. Here are some examples of the extent to which the computer, old-style, has replaced people by devouring our mountains of routine clerical work.

First, the football pools – a British gambling obsession shared by only a few countries, Australia, Canada and Sweden among them. Every Monday morning in the football season the checking machines at Vernons Pools are quietly killing punters' dreams at a rate of 15,000 coupons an hour; women at 120 keyboard terminals in three barn-like factories around the fringes of Liverpool are talking to the central computer, entering details of the few winners who got Saturday's football results right, and plucking out those clients' accounts; and in the locked, air-conditioned, old-style computer room the compact printing machines are idling at routine tasks, waiting to write about 25,000 cheques the next day. That pressurized process points all the lessons:

Employment cut by more than fifty per cent within a decade. The jobs that have gone were the epitome of boredom – but who gets the economic benefits?

Much faster operation, fewer errors, greater security – and that increased breadth is combined with the depth of fingertip access to a huge collection of data. Physical sorting of millions of coupons every week has been eliminated; acres of card indexes of customers' accounts have been abandoned.

And the need for centralized operation has gone – the three operating centres are joined by land-line. Were it not for receiving the bets, the computers could just as well be in Taiwan.

About the only thing not automated is the calculation of the pool dividend – the winnings. 'The accountants guard that jealously,' according to Vernons' computer manager; though 'they've probably got as far as using a calculator.'

Vernons' began using computers in a small way in 1965. The first use of remote terminals was in 1971 and the present system has been operating since 1976. There are now fewer than 3000 employees – ninety-six per cent of them women and fifty per cent of them part-timers (there are no women in upper management). The halving of the staff has come gradually, through natural wastage, and the firm claims that with current labour costs there would be no business without automation.

For those still employed, the computer has made work easier, but it still looks a dismal way in which to have to spend a large chunk of one's life. The women who work the computer terminals have fifteen weeks' training. They sit in serried rows and are not allowed to talk. The normal shift is from 8.30 a.m. to 6 p.m. but the spells of work at the terminals are not supposed to exceed two hours without a break.

The routine checking of the coupons is done by OCR (optical character recognition) machines, which work in the same way, basically, as the laser-scan supermarket check-outs described in Chapter 7. These machines can, in theory, check the bets at a rate of 24,000 an hour. In practice, the coupons go along the conveyor belt to oblivion at only 15,000 an hour, to allow for manual stacking, the occasional blockage, and the even more occasional bell that signals a winner. The machines have to deal with more than two million bets within ten hours. As the coupons speed along the belt they pass over a light source. There they are read by an array of ninety silicon cells. That process covers more than eighty per cent of the coupons. The rest of the bets – those that go in for involved permutations – are dealt with on the computer terminals or by a small residue of manual checkers.

The OCR machines are linked to a room of mini-computers which also run the microfilming process. All the coupons are microfilmed (at a rate of 40,000 an hour) as soon as they arrive. This is done so that no one can fiddle the bets within Vernons.

The 15,000-an-hour rate for checking the coupons compares with a top human rate of about 500 an hour, and, of course, there are now fewer errors: the number of protest claims has dropped by twenty-five per cent. That 15,000 to 500 comparison vastly understates the case, because it does not include the enormous job in the old days of sorting the coupons into categories and postal areas. Every client then had an index card, which needed to be updated every week. The computers now do the sorting and update and store the account information. (A side bonus here is the ability to send propaganda letters automatically to punters who have drifted away.) Clients' records are found among the millions in the computer store by a simple index – the first three letters of the surname, the first three letters of the street name. The details then appear on the screen of the computer terminal in blocks of four – and the system hits the nail first time in 99·7 per cent of cases. In the other 0·3 per cent, the required account is virtually certain to appear in the second block of four.

The system includes a number of accuracy as well as security checks. For instance, if the operator is dealing with a coupon making forty selections but she keys in only thirty-nine, the computer checks with its record of that coupon and a message appears on the screen telling her to start again.

Just to show the universality of this old-hat use of the computer to replace mundane clerical work, here is an example less than 200 miles from industrial Liverpool, yet two nations apart. These computers are in an eighteenth-century mansion, set in parkland, complete with meandering stream. Scotsbridge House at Rickmansworth, Hertfordshire, headquarters of the British Friesian Cattle Society, has more of the atmosphere of a country hotel than of an office.

The society's chief executive, Major-General Derek Pounds, ex-Royal Marines, estimates that the computer has saved the society between £70,000 and £90,000 a year – ten per cent of its expenditure. Those savings are divided between increased efficiency and reduced staff. Pounds says that without computerization of the society's records, he would need a staff of 200 today, but 120 are now enough – and 40 of those are part-timers, again mainly women.

A central part of the society's work is providing the Somerset House of the breed, and the computer has been handling that since 1975. (An indication of the global-village aspects of computing is that an identical system has been used by the Australian Kennel Club since 1977.) The records of 1·8 million Friesians, owned by 14,000 members of the society, are available on the system's display terminals; and 180,000 new registrations are dealt with every year. The computer can provide pedigrees three generations deep, detailing what General Pounds calls 'the batting average'. Those pedigrees deal not only in parentage and ownership but with blood types, milk yields, and predicted breeding values. The society handles 5000 registrations a week at peak periods. In the days of index cards, it took four or five months to reply; now the average is three days, though a backlog of two or three weeks can develop at the height of the calving rush. But the five million historical records still exist, in a roomful of card-index cabinets. The reason is that the record of each animal includes a drawing of its markings. Those drawings are now being microfilmed. The alternative of using a pattern-recognition system (a more intricate version of Vernon's conveyor-belt scanning) to put the details straight into the computer was not considered, mainly because of cost.

Another major saving in cost and time has been achieved in publishing the society's annual breed book. This richly bound Who's Who of Friesians costs £8·50 and about a thousand copies are sold each year. Pre-computer, that job cost £40,000 a year and occupied a full-time staff of six. Now a computer tape is sent to the printers and the book is printed directly from that. The work costs £12,000 – and without the staff of six.

That brings us to the next stage, the explosive stage: the computer replacing the craftsman and the manager. The printer makes a better example of this than, say, the watchmaker, for a number of reasons.

First, it did not need the arrival of the microprocessor for the craftsman to be replaced. The process began in the United States in the early 1970s with orthodox computers and by 1977 ninety per cent of US newspapers were computer-printed. Therefore, we are still dealing, as at Vernons' and Scotsbridge House, with the basic principle – the capabilities of the computer without the added strengths of compactness and reduced capital costs provided by the chip.

Second, the newspaper industry was probably the first in which it could be demonstrated that it would make balance-sheet sense to pay people for life to go away and leave it to the machine. That is theory no longer. After the horrendous confrontations of the early years, a number of American papers have settled with the printing union on that basis: the choice of pay for life without work or lump-sum redundancy. Microelectronics is rapidly extending the range of industries where that would be feasible.

Third, what has happened to the printer is beginning to happen to the typist. An essential component of the automated office is the word-processor, the microcomputer that replaces the typewriter; and the computer terminals that newspaper reporters use are, in essence, word-processors.

Fourth, the switching of a newspaper on to the computer is so complicated a process that it illuminates most of the standard problems: the need for immaculate attention to detail so that no apparently minor but in fact essential detail of the old methods is blurred in the new; equally, the need for imaginative planning so that opportunities are not lost by producing an electronic operation that merely apes the old mechanical one; and the need for mutual education, then close liaison, between the systems analysts devising the computer system and the people who will manage and use it.

And, fifth: the newspaper shows that the employment implications of automation go deeper than the craftsman; it can make economic sense to cut management and journalistic employment as well.

The financial logic of computer-printing is indisputable. Even in 1976, the Royal Commission on the Press demonstrated that Britain's national daily papers could be prepared for press five times faster and with an overall annual saving of about £35 millions – all that for a one-off payment of £55 millions, including redundancy payments to perhaps 7000 printers. It is the ultimate example of the British disease that four years later more than half those papers are still produced by the old methods – and that even those using the computer do so on the basis of printers still retyping what journalists have already typed.

That was the crucial issue of the long closure of *The Times*; for, once the reporter is working at a computer terminal instead of a typewriter, there is no reason for his words to be retyped – the words are already in the computer ready for printing. Fleet Street, therefore, lives with the absurdity of thousands of people travelling daily through the rush-hour traffic to do a job that is not only no longer necessary but is arguably counter-productive.

The immediate gains that the computer brings to the newspaper can be summarized in two comparisons:

1. The 'quality' daily papers (those with more text than pictures) each need five hours' work, or more, from between 100 and 200 production men to prepare an edition for the presses in the old ways – from the first setting into type of the day's news until the final page of the night's first edition is ready for conversion into a printing plate. And that only covers the current pages of the night; feature and advertisement pages occupy the daytime or late-night shifts. One computer-driven photosetter, the size of a wardrobe, can do all that in less than an hour.

2. One keyboard operator, using a traditional typesetting machine, would need about an hour to set into type one column of news – with, inevitably, a few errors which would have to be corrected later. One photosetter can produce the whole page, seven or eight columns, in around a minute, with errors eliminated beforehand.

Photocomposition is the central ally of the computer in printing. The former hot-metal method of printing usually involves producing every line of a newspaper on a typesetting machine that has remained essentially unchanged since its development in the 1880s: a keyboard machine moulds the letters on semi-molten metal to produce a solid slug of metal, which represents one line in a newspaper column. These lines are then collected and put in the page by hand. In photocomposition – cold printing – a photosetter takes the words from the computer and puts them on film, and that film is used to produce the printing plate.

Much of the material in a daily paper produced by the old methods undergoes at least eight processes, involving six different groups of workers, before the words approach a printing press. Some of those words are 'retyped' four times as they progress along the chain. And, if you include the movement around the place of thousands of bits of paper and chunks of metal type, the total number of operations per article can top twenty. Along that chain the buck never stops. Errors are inevitably introduced in following and refollowing the words on grubby slips of much-handled paper – and the correcting of those errors often succeeds only in introducing new errors.

The computer can reduce that nonsense to two human operations: the writing, then the editing. And, if there are errors, those errors can be traced to the individual journalist. In a computerized newspaper office nothing need appear on paper. The computer terminal that replaces the reporter's typewriter shows the words on a screen above the keyboard as the reporter types. The only significant variation from the office typist's word-processor is that the screen also tells the writer how many words he has written and how much space those words would occupy in the paper.

The writer can rearrange words or phrases, correct spelling errors or delete whole paragraphs, and the computer will keep him constant company, instantly readjusting the spacing of the lines and still recording at the top of the screen the changing total numbers of words or the number of column millimetres they would occupy in the paper. And, as we have already seen, those computer terminals are not office-bound. Reporters can keyboard straight into the computer's memory from football stadium or courthouse or hotel bedroom. The *New York Times* began using them across the Atlantic, from London and Paris, in 1976: yes, 1976.

Editing is also accomplished on computer terminals. Instead of struggling through an ocean of paper, the person in charge of a particular page can tell the computer to supply him with a directory of all the material available. He can then, by pushing another key or two, direct on to the screen those pieces he needs.

In many newspapers at present all this computery ends in a shameful parody of traditional printing methods. Paper strips of the columns of photoset material are pasted on a board, in the same fashion as columns of metal type used to be fitted into a page.

Equipment that eliminates this manual fiddling has been available since around 1976 but there is still some editorial argument about its ease of use. These page-editing terminals offer the editor the whole page on the screen, and the reports for that page are slotted into place by keyboard instructions or light pencils. The computer then photosets the whole page.

This is another area where the newspaper provides a microcosm of the wider process. Computers used in design are replacing the skills of the draughtsman, just as they replace the skills of the printer. We have seen that already in the design of the silicon chip itself, and it is becoming apparent over wide areas, from the management of huge chemical plants to the design of shoes. In a chemical plant or oil refinery it is possible to store all the blueprints in a computer system. You can then call to the screen any section of the pipeline, make the computer show it to you from several angles, then reshape it. Similar techniques are used in the bigger architectural partnerships, and the microcomputer and cheaper micro-run digitizers (which transfer maps and drawings into digital form) are now bringing them to the smaller architects' office. When town planners want to change the scale of a map, it can take a draughtsman four days; the computer does it in a few minutes.

The newspaper also illustrates an adjoining effect of the computer: the removal of skills from some of the craft jobs that remain. In Britain, many local papers, while using the computer years ahead of Fleet Street, have done so in compromise fashion by leaving the work-division between printer and journalist largely untouched. The printers still employed are then often doing different, more mundane work.

Keyboard operators, working on the old hot-metal machines, made a significant contribution to the appearance of the page. Their skill included spacing the words on the lines, to avoid splitting words at the ends of lines or making those splits easy on the reader when they did occur. Today the computer does that, and all the keyboard operator does is bash out the words as fast as he can. And through cost-cutting (or through failure to understand what the computer needs to be told about the strange constructions of the English language) many newspaper computers do that job badly.

The compositors who constructed the pages from those lines of metal type contributed equally to the appearance of the pages, through subtle balancing of the white space in headlines and between lines of text. Now the computer does that during the filming process – and, again, can do it badly if the typographical wisdom it is supplied with is not sufficiently comprehensive.

Another example of the ubiquity of computer technology, bringing similar advantages and problems to many industries, is newspaper use of a more sophisticated relative of the docfax described in Chapter 8. This form of electronic transmission is used to send newspaper pages to several printing centres, improving distribution to the customer and reducing the duplication of printing and editorial staffs at those sub-centres.

The technique was first used in the 1950s. It has spread in the familiar pattern, cheaper and faster equipment making it more economic. The introduction of data compression, the same advance that produced high-speed docfax, enables a broadsheet newspaper page to be transmitted, by land-line or radio, in four minutes – it used to take half an hour per page. The essential difference between this and the ordinary commercial uses of docfax is quality: the detail has to be fine enough for a laser beam at the receiving end to transfer the information to a sheet of photographic film that will produce a printing plate of the same quality as the original.

The method is used to provide simultaneous editions in different countries – for instance, by the *Financial Times* (London to Frankfurt), the *Herald-Tribune* (Paris to London), and by the *Wall Street Journal*, over satellite, to several printing centres. Another increasing use, particularly in the United States, is to supply papers with a method of overcoming the death of the inner cities by printing at satellite plants in the prosperous suburbs.

The computer in the newspaper does not, of course, serve editorial-cum-production needs alone. Parallel procedures are used for advertisements. Then there are the general commercial uses of the computer on the management and accountancy sides. Computers are also used to monitor the high-speed presses and to automate the packing and dispatching of papers. Methods are being developed to eliminate the cumbersome collection of processes involved in making a printing plate. One is for the computer to transfer its information direct on to a plate through a laser beam; another is to do without a plate altogether by directing jets of ink straight on to the paper.

Ink-jet printing has been available in principle for about eighty years but only recently has microelectronics made it practicable. So far its main use has been in marking goods for the food and packaging industries, where it can print on a knobbly bag of potatoes as well as on a box of chocolates. Its next advance looks likely to be in high-speed printing for office word-processor systems. Its advantages to newspapers will be that the words can be changed without stopping the presses – the computer just orders a change in the shape of the millions of minute specks of ink bombarding the paper.

Before that happens – and perhaps before Fleet Street sorts itself out – the newspaper, in printed form at least, may disappear altogether under the waves of viewdata networks.

Before we leave the newspaper world, there are a few more present realities to mention. First, it needs to be said that the sanguine view I have presented of the editorial advantages of the computer is by no means shared by all. The strongest argument of the advocates of gradual change is that a daily paper cannot afford to miss a day's issue because in the newspaper industry, unlike other industries, the revenue lost is a total loss. And whoever heard of a complex computer system that operated flawlessly from Day One?

Editorially, there are powerful voices which say that the computer does not yet match the detailed editing requirements of a British newspaper. The core of the argument here is that what has worked well in the US will not work in the UK, because American papers are often less tightly edited and designed and show less typographical flair and care. There is concern, too, about the problems of rapid consultation, where decisions are made by shuffling bits of paper across the desk, amalgamating and re-amalgamating multiple versions of one major story.

These criticisms need to be balanced against the American experience. On American metropolitan dailies there is grassroots editorial enthusiasm. It centres on the ease and speed of writing on the computer terminal; the automatic accuracy of story length; and, above all, on a fierce sense of ultimate responsibility. In the old days, the *Baltimore Sun* averaged a thousand misprints in its first edition of the night: now that the journalists themselves are responsible for the final accuracy of what they type, the early-edition

111

misprints average fewer than forty.

Yet most of those papers' computer systems ape the editorial patterns of operation that grew up with – and were to some extent governed by – the constraints of hot-metal printing. There is little evidence of newspaper people first learning what the computer will enable them to do, then ignoring what went on before, and thinking solely of how to use the computer's capabilities to produce the end-product they actually want. The lack of that lateral thinking is apparent in a host of computer systems in commerce and industry. The computer people often cannot produce it because they do not know all the details of the business using their computers; and the users cannot do it unless they are prepared to learn about computers.

Apply virgin thinking to newspapers and you begin to realize that many journalists' jobs could be as unnecessary as the printers', if your sole concern is to produce a competitive product at minimum cost. Which brings us to the final object-lesson from the newspaper: the logic of automation extends deep into the territory of so-called brainwork, and will go deeper.

The simplest example is a newspaper's production management team. Most of their time and overtime is spent on labour relations. No staff – no job. But there are still machines to be monitored and updated? One man pulling out a dud circuit board and plugging in a new one covers much of the first problem; you call in the computer consultants for the second. That argument extends into many of those middle jobs where executives prepare advice for top management. In producing financial analyses and manipulating economic models, the computer does that too.

There this chapter comes almost full circle: from the earliest computer consumption of routine clerical work, like the company payroll, to the decision-making regions. What remains to close the circle is the total management system, running the automated office and the robot factory. Even that may soon be approaching the point of balance – the point at which, if we find we cannot cope socially or technically, it will be too late to turn back.

10. Jobs that are going

The public-relations phrase is The Office Of The Future, and, like many PR phrases, it hides a truth. Most of the elements of the automated office have been around for years, as we have seen. Microelectronics has made it economic to employ them more fully and to knit them into a cohesive whole. The aim is the virtual abolition of paper-passing; and, as in the newspaper, the key is the word-processor that replaces the typewriter.

But there is one important difference between the newspaper and the general office world: most journalists type their own reports, whereas most office workers do not type their own letters and memoranda. Many of the firms competing to supply the tools of office automation admit that this could be one of the brakes on the rate of change. For total automation to be achieved – where the only human element left is the decision-making element – the boss himself must use the computer, and that looks likely to happen only when he no longer has to tinker with a keyboard but can chat directly with the machine and forget about the power-symbolism of the secretary. And many computer scientists say that that real ability to talk to computers will begin to be practicable by about 1985.

The logic of automation eventually replacing most servant jobs is demonstrated by one of the minor accessories of the process. This is a computer that understands handwriting, and it encapsulates most of the lessons of the silicon chip: it uses microelectronics to make an invention smaller, smarter, surer – and much cheaper; its life should be short by old-world standards – machines that may make it redundant were emerging before it even started work; and it cuts out the duplicating, error-provoking, delaying middleman jobs.

It's called a Micropad. You write on it with ballpoint pen or pencil and the computer gets the message by interpreting the pressure on the pad. The idea was first developed at the British Government's National Physical Laboratory at Teddington. It was then taken up by one of those small, pioneering companies – Quest Automation, at Ferndown in Dorset – which in 1975 made a version called Datapad. That machine did not have a microprocessor on board; it needed an expensive outside computer to run it. Therefore, a system using eight pads cost £40,000 – Micropad costs £1725 per pad.

Micropad can be used more easily, for a wider range of jobs, than Datapad, and it is slightly less fussy about the quality of handwriting (as you write, the words appear on a small screen at the top of the pad, for checking). But it still deals only in capital letters, though it recognizes common symbols, like +, −, or £. Its obvious use remains with standard forms, such as invoices, but it could also be used to write and dispatch Telex messages; or, as part of a word-processing system, to order routine letters to be printed automatically.

But the real point about Micropad is that – in limited areas – it makes it easier for the executive to deal directly with the computer without having to worry about keyboard skills. Quest Automation make no bones about the employment implications. They say that Telex procedures in many companies are farcical – messages copied by secretaries from manager's scrawls, then carried around the building, then joining a queue on the Telex operator's desk ,just to be copied again, perhaps incorrectly. Micropad, at £1725 a go, could add to the small but growing number of cases where it could still be commercially profitable if people were paid for life not to work.

Word-processing does not bite as deep as that. Unless managers become enamoured of the tricks that the computerized typewriter can play, there will be typing pools and secretaries for years to come – though, inevitably, fewer of them.

There is, though, one device that just might hasten the process long before the voice computer becomes firmly established. It is a pocket typewriter invented by an American film director, Cy Endfield, whose dabblings in microelectronics began as a hobby. His Microwriter has gone into production with backing from the Hambros merchant banking group. It looks like a pocket calculator, except that it has only five keys. These keys form the letters in combination; hence it is a substitute not for the dictating machine but for the pen. Some people have learnt how to use it within an hour.

The five keys are placed in the pattern of a set of finger prints, and the letters are produced by pressing keys simultaneously in the basic shape of the letter. For example, the letter 'l' is produced by pressing the thumb and index finger, which corresponds to the vertical line of an 'l'. The words appear, twelve letters at a time, on a calculator-style display strip. The machine's memory chips can hold seven or eight single-page business letters, and extra storage is provided by cassettes. The Microwriter does not itself produce words on paper. It plugs into an electronic typewriter or a computer system – by phone line, if the user is travelling. For home use, a black box has been developed so that the words can appear on an ordinary TV screen.

Voice communication with the computer has begun – both ways – but such systems are still in infancy. This might be the best point at which to break briefly with the strictly office theme and take a look at them.

Computers that can interpret the voice have been mainly used, so far, in jobs where people are too busy using their hands, moving goods or checking documents, to tap a keyboard as well. Mostly, the computer is given simple instructions by number. One example is postal sorting; another is checking goods in and out of warehouses. An American company, Threshold, has produced computers which understand a thousand words, and has used them to enable a totally disabled person to steer an electric-powered wheelchair through voice commands. Home microcomputers which will obey simple instructions given through the microphone are also on sale. The matching brand of computers that themselves talk tend, in business use, to use the recorded human voice, rather than a synthetic version. Among the first industries to see their advantages were the car manufacturers, who use them for communication around their national dealer networks, but they are also getting into the mail-order and food trades.

Ford UK use one of these 'voice-response' systems to link 550 dealers to a spare-parts centre at Daventry, Northants. The computer voice that the dealers hear over the phone line belongs to an American actress, Jacqueline Rowan, who recorded the system's 129-word vocabulary. The choice of Rowan was something of a concession to jingoism : both Ford and Menzies (the company supplying the system) like to emphasize that she has worked a lot in Britain and talks real English – 'firmly Home Counties'.

The computer terminal used by the dealers is the size of a portable typewriter. The order or query is put to the central computer via the keyboard and the computer's answer – which it chooses from the collection of recorded stock phrases – is relayed through a built-in loudspeaker to the left of the keyboard. For travelling salesmen there is a pocket version, with a cup to put over the phone earpiece.

The Daventry centre holds 85,000 types of vehicle parts, and orders are received from dealers at a rate of 5000 parts an hour. Once the computer has checked the security code of the caller, it will give him details of any change in the part number required, confirmation that the part is available on the depot shelves, and the latest price. It will also check that dealers do not omit important ordering details. And it can handle twenty-four calls at once.

A similar system provides weather reports to airline pilots approaching Heathrow Airport, London, but this time the voice is military – that of Colonel John West of the Marconi company. He has recorded a collection of standard weather phrases, words and figures, and the computer plucks the appropriate bits from its memory as it reads incoming weather reports. It then broadcasts summaries on four radio frequencies.

The genuine computer voice, concocted by the silicon chip, still tends to have Dalek overtones. But the Japanese company Toshiba boasts that its talking TV set has 'a sweet feminine voice'. This gimmick, of which test models were shown at the 1979 Japan Electronics Show in Osaka, is typical of the way in which the synthetic voice is finding an opening in consumer products. The set's microcomputer accepts about thirty simple voice commands – 'Channel Three, please', 'Switch off' – and says 'OK' for message received and understood. If it is baffled, the computer says 'Once more, please'. But the need for such repetitions, even when two people are instructing the set, is said to be less than five per cent. The voice recognition takes one second and the set obeys half a second later.

Texas Instruments have marketed a hand-held talking computer that teaches children to spell, and, in Japan, Sharp have produced a desktop calculator which speaks English, French, German, Spanish and, of course, Japanese – though you will only get one language per calculator. Here, the synthetic voice tolls the process of your calculation (arithmetical terms as well as numbers) and it is possible to adjust the speed at which it speaks.

More significantly, IBM have introduced a voice synthesizer for their magnetic-card typewriters, to enable blind typists to check their own work. The unit reads back the contents of the magnetic cards, spelling out words if necessary, and telling the typist the point he has reached on the page. Another way in which the voice is being introduced to word-processors is through the vocal footnote. The idea here is that the manager sending an important memo by electronic mail will instruct the computer to give it a voiced alert at the end – 'You must look at this, Fred.'

However, the current motivations for automating the office have little to do with such possibilities. The trigger word is productivity. The jumble of interests that are pushing the total office system – long-established computer companies, big telecommunications and electronics groups getting in on the office-computer act, and a host of smaller, often new firms making the ever-cheaper chip-run word-processors themselves – all make the propaganda point that computers cut office costs. They note that while investment in manufacturing plant and process-industry equipment has been raising production efficiency for decades, investment in the office has stagnated. Back in 1978, when the electronics group Plessey announced their all-digital private phone exchanges, projected as providing the communications centre of the computerized office, they emphasized one statistic: eighty-five per cent of office costs go in wages. Similar figures have often been used since. Microcomputer systems to control hotel administration have been advertised on the basis that the capital costs can be recouped in nine months, the savings splitting about 50-50 between increased efficiency and staff cuts.

One of the few independent reports on the effectiveness of the word-processor has said that suppliers' claims of one hundred per cent overall increases in office productivity need to be treated with caution. A study published by the British government department which advises Whitehall on computers welcomed the word-processor, but not ecstatically.

The report covered the findings of a one-year pilot project at the Darlington offices of the Department of Education and Science. The workrate of word-processors was compared with that of electric typewriters, and the conclusion was that, because of the cost of buying and maintaining the equipment, word-processing was not more cost-effective than the existing methods for the overall mix of work in the Darlington typing pool. (But many British offices are still stuck with mechanical typewriters, anyway. Also, the average age of the typists on the trial was forty-six – hardly typical.)

The report said that the general indication was that the gains from word-processing were well worthwhile, provided that the work was carefully selected and the aptitude of individual typists taken into account. Word-processors were 'highly advantageous' – between 200 and 400 per cent more productive than electric typewriters – for material which went through a number of drafting stages, because of the ease with which text could be juggled on the screen.

That is an aspect of the word-processor that needs underlining. Many of the machines in use today are not bought to provide electronic mail around a vast company network. They stand alone in small offices, joined only to a printer, and their usefulness, apart from the easy editing and speed of typing, can lie in the way in which names and addresses can be added swiftly to circular letters to make them look personal. And the best of them are truly computers, with multiple uses. Bath Technical College has used one word-processor to build a databank (stored on disc) of 600 questions for use in a physics course; to draw up the college timetables; to compile and print the thirty-four-page internal phone directory; and to edit and print a college news sheet.

Estimates of the number of word-processors in the United

States vary from half a million up to nearly a million. West Germany was estimated to have 55,000 in mid-1979, France 28,000, and Britain 23,000. The leading microelectronics analysts, Mackintosh Consultants, have said that their use in Europe will expand by twenty-seven per cent a year through the early 1980s; and Erv Stedman, president of the American-based user group, the International Word-Processing Association, says that US sales are rising at a rate of thirty per cent a year.

The UK's National Computing Centre has calculated that, with such rates of sales, the price of a communicating word-processor will have fallen by seventy to eighty per cent before 1987. The NCC theorizes that the tentative progress into office automation in Britain has been driven not by the logic of greater efficiency but by the shortage of secretaries, the cost of office space, and the reduction in the quality of the postal service. Stedman claims that word-processors have already brought wider opportunities for women to move into management, partly because secretaries can reduce the typing part of their work to a brief side-line.

Of course, word-processors are only one part, though a crucial part, of the so-called Office Of The Future. The major commercial struggle is between the big groups competing to provide the total package with all the elements we have discussed – digital communications through computerized company phone exchanges; office computers that no longer restrict themselves to the payrolls, the balance sheets, and the bills but organize databanks of all the company's information and make that information available on desktop terminals (if you are high enough on the tree to be given the passwords); plus all the bits and pieces, like radio bleepers and security clocking-in cards, which can now be computer-controlled.

Mackintosh Consultants reckon that the number of office computers in Europe will increase at a rate of forty-seven per cent a year till 1983 – and that about seventy per cent of those new computers will be for small office systems, used entirely by laymen with no computer professionals around.

That process could make the computer journeyman himself redundant; the computer is no respecter of its friends. As the computer terminal becomes as common in the office as the phone, as the computer itself gets smaller and less in need of tender air-conditioning to help it keep cool, so the mystical aura of the computer department will dissolve – there will be no computer department. First to go will be the computer operators; then the computer managers; then, probably, the programmers, as companies increasingly accept the package solution for routine uses of the computer (though, even in individual user-company terms, the programmer has a long way to go – in fact, today there is an horrendous world-wide shortage of them).

One home-to-roost aspect of this is that some old-school managements have tended in the past to look on the people who run their computers – the data-processing managers – as second-level technicians, slotting them into the same mental category as the factory foreman. And, in some cases, that's what they have got in consequence – the bright sparks have learnt the lesson and hurried off to better prospects. And now that computers are becoming omnipresent in companies, and managing directors and chairmen hurry off on 'computer appreciation' courses, those companies, in their search for an overall policy and a computing supremo, are turning to management consultants rather than their own computer people.

This tendency has so alarmed the Institute of Data-Processing Management in Britain that its secretary-general, Ted Cluff, has warned his members that 'if they put their heads under the bedclothes and say it won't happen to them, then they are in danger.' Cluff admits that the computer profession has begun to breed its own Luddites.

He says data-processing managers have failed to meet the challenges of the chip in a number of areas. He is particularly concerned about the gap that could develop between the traditional computer people in the offices and the engineers involved with the fresher uses of the microcomputer, in automating production lines and updating products.

Strangely, the office-factory link has not been much emphasized, although factory management information systems are expanding, too. One would imagine that it would be attractive to top management to have all the strings extending to their office terminals, so that they could as easily check the day's progress on the assembly lines as look up yesterday's sales figures.

One of the companies that has said it is aiming at this overall approach is also one of the companies using the convergence of telecommunications, general electronics and computing to challenge the traditional computer suppliers in the office world. It is Racal, an electronics group that has previously concentrated on the heavier end, specializing in military communications. It has formed a subsidiary to design and make chip-based office systems and plans to extend that involvement to unite them with the monitoring of automated factories and warehouses.

Most of the academic, union and government reports forecasting what the chip will accomplish in the 1980s emphasize the changes in the office. By contrast, the impact of microelectronics on manufacturing industry will, they say, be relatively small. Iann Barron and Ray Curnow, in their massive report to the British government, commissioned from the science policy research unit at Sussex University by the Department of Industry, said that electronic information systems would totally replace paper work within ten to fifteen years. But they concluded that factory automation would continue to develop piecemeal – and slowly – because this would reduce job upsets and because a big return on investment was unlikely.

They seem tactfully to be saying that – in Britain, anyway – unions are not only stronger in the factories but that the shop-floor is also more resistant to change. Yet it is not entirely the high-wage economies that are now taking with alacrity to the industrial robot.

11. The real robots

Industrial robots are not new, not remotely humanoid, and not even numerous (up to now). Again, the universal point has to be made: factory automation was underway well before Charlie Chaplin's horror story, *Modern Times*; post-war, it was boosted and broadened by those clumsier computers producing a premature furore about peopleless factories; now the chip has removed most of the remaining technical and economic barriers, and the peopleless factories are there, if only in experimental form.

In industry, the old computers did best in controlling flows rather than running robots, and chemical plants and oil refineries have been highly automated for years. But the chip has had a big influence there, too. Monitoring a big chemical plant in pre-micro days involved a control room with, maybe, a 140-foot stretch of dials and displays. Now it can come down to two colour-TV screens and a couple of dozen buttons, producing a flood of real-time statistics and moving diagrams.

The pattern has been similar on the factory assembly line. For years, industrial robots have been bulky (most of them look like tank turrets, with an arm replacing the gun), have needed separate computers to run them, and have been best at heavy jobs such as welding car bodies. The chip has made them smaller, cleverer and more independent; and the general-purpose robot, which can be programmed for a number of tasks, has arrived.

Calculations of the numbers of robots in the world's factories are bedevilled by the problem of definition: when does a bit of mechanical-cum-electronic machinery cross the borderline of robotics by becoming capable of copying human functions? Using the strictest criteria, Tom Brock, secretary of the British Robot Association, made a world survey in 1979 which produced a total of under 9000 – Japan in front with 4500, the United States next with 2000, West Germany 600 (thirty per cent of the European total), Italy 400, and Britain 130 (where there were fewer than 80 a year before). But broader-based calculations have given Japan alone a total of 16,000, with a production rate of 3000 a year. The world total of machines that manipulate tools and materials must be well over 80,000.

On broad definitions, industrial robots range in size from primitive hands (called pick-and-place units), which humbly move components from place to place, to huge lifting frames, fifteen feet tall or more, which carry heavy machinery around without human guidance (except in their pre-programming, of course). Robots used to be used mainly for spot-welding and paint-spraying, and predominantly in the motor industry. Their role has now expanded into arc-welding, running machine tools and general assembly-line work.

Those robots requiring snaky arms – to reach the awkward corners of a car body or to spray paint on a chair – used to be taught their jobs by being physically led through the motions by the skilled human worker. That precise sequence of movements was then recorded in the computer memories. Now most robots can be programmed from a hand-held keypad.

A good example of the new generation, run by the microprocessor, is a robot designed to work side by side with people on any factory line assembling smallish parts. It is simply an arm and a hand on top of a box. It can position objects to an accuracy of 0·004 of an inch and can move five ways – corresponding to the human waist, shoulder, elbow, wrist and hand rotation. That robot, called Puma (another of those awful acronyms – programmable universal manipulator for assembly), is made by Unimation, an American company that was a pioneer and is still the leader in making robots. Puma is being used for such intricate jobs as putting the lights in car instrument panels.

The moral case for the industrial robot has always been devastating. It works faster and more accurately than people in boring, grotty, sometimes dangerous jobs. It never gets tired and rarely sick, it needs no holidays, it knows nothing of Monday-morning-hangover carelessness, or Friday-afternoon euphoria. But, until now, in our brutal world, people have generally been cheaper. The chip has changed that.

Here is a routine example. Fujitsu Fanuc, in Japan, make a robot which feeds and manages automated machine tools. It's not new, it is one of the orthodox tank-turret machines. Its arms are not flexible, because they don't need to be. Its job is to pick up a wide variety of components and pass them to the machine tools in the right sequence and at the right time. Its hands have sensors which will stop the work and call for human help if they detect an error. It can run five different machine tools at once. It is not cheap – one of the ways it is being sold in Europe is in a £60,000 package, which includes maintenance and supervisor training. Yet one of those robots will do the work of several men for a pay rate of £1 an hour. That raw calculation is based on the price, on performance and reliability claims, and on the assumption that the robot works for ten years (some have already been working longer), for a mere twenty hours a day, and for only 300 days a year.

Of course, there are severe restrictions on the industrial robot's current capabilities and, as with almost anything to do with the computer, teething troubles have abounded. Even in the robot-hungry car industry, the human hand is still required on the final assembly line.

Cars are not yet 'hand-built by robots', as Fiat have

127

claimed in a series of seductive television advertisements, but Fiat have gone further than most in the Robogate lines at their Rivalta factory in Turin and at Cassino in southern Italy. The robot welding lines there cost about thirty per cent more than old-fashioned lines but need only 25 supervisory workers, compared with 125 before. They also enable the mix of models (three-door or five-door) to be switched easily to match demand. Fiat claim that the early hiccoughs – which caused one plant director to complain that robots 'have not been a good experience' – are firmly over.

The British car industry employed one of the earliest industrial robots. It was installed at Cowley in 1968 and still works there on a sub-assembly line. But over the decade when the robot spread from the United States and Japan to the car factories of France, Germany, Sweden and Italy, British Leyland just tinkered with three more. At last it has bought twenty-eight to run the car-body assembly of the new Metro model. Fiat now have more than 200 robots and Volkswagen more than 100 – and in both cases some of them have been built by their own machine-tool subsidiary companies and are being sold to other firms. Five years ago West Germany had no robot-making firms; now there are a dozen.

Those figures demonstrate the Catch 22 aspects of drifting behind the international competition. The robot is finally catching on across British industry. It looks as though the numbers employed could double every year till the mid-1980s – yet about eighty per cent of those new robots will probably have to be imported. The reason is not lack of robotics expertise but lack of a previous home market. Britain has one small firm making robots – Hall Automation, at Watford – making about two robots a week and exporting well over half of them. Now that a home demand has arrived, Unimation is moving into UK manufacture, Hall Automation has been taken over by the biggest British electronics group, GEC, and a couple of other small

128

companies are emerging – years too late.

A common theory for the varying national responses to automation pinpoints social attitudes. John Meleka, the Egyptian-born technology director of British Leyland, in discussing why the British car industry has been sluggish about it, puts the argument this way: in the United States, workers are dollar-dominated; in Japan, there is absolute dedication and discipline (and, he might have added, a national strategy, involving huge public investment and close liaison between government and industry); in Western Europe, there are the migrant workers, 'well-disciplined, under six-month contracts'; but the British worker is 'more socially and intellectually advanced'.

Meleka says that this will work to Britain's advantage in time, because it will become increasingly difficult for any country to capture the sort of labour that is ready for repetitive production-line work. Car-union leaders and Meleka are unanimous in the phrase they choose to describe the average production job in the motor industry: soul-destroying.

Many of the jobs on manual assembly lines are obviously of life-or-death importance to the driver who buys that car, yet they consist of doing the same thing, every hour, every day. The sort of group-working pioneered by the Swedes can only be a palliative. The most horrific areas are the paint shops. Even in one of Leyland's latest plants – the Rover line built at a cost of £94 millions on the outskirts of Solihull – the final touches of paint were still, in 1979, sprayed on to the car interiors by people – working, masked, in glass cages.

Experimental factories where the only human workers are a few roving technicians have been established in several countries – even Bulgaria. The Japanese Industry Ministry has indicated that the Japanese target is to have unmanned factories in general use by 1990. These plants often depend not only on robots but on a sister technology

which is probably more significant in the immediate term –
the computer-managed machine tool.

These techniques (called numerical control) began twenty-
five years ago, just when an ally was being developed in the
uses of the computer in design of machine parts – and, of
course, the chip has enlivened both the machine tools and
computer graphics. The United States is not so far behind
Japan here. The McDonnell Douglas factory in St Louis
has about two dozen acres of unattended milling machines,
grinding the patterns into aircraft parts to an accuracy of
0·0025 of an inch. The few people wandering around are
either engineers, taking the occasional glance at a control
panel, or less fortunate people sweeping the cuttings – and
the accuracy of automation means that there are fewer
cuttings to sweep. The sort of wandering robot which took
over the domestic round for Jane Babbage could become
cheap enough before 1990 to take over such factory chores.
They exist at present only in the laboratories. But their
precursors are appearing in public, in one or two offices,
delivering the mail, or coping with terrorist bombs in the
street.

In fact, the free-wheeling, multi-armed robot that knows
its master's voice will be moving from the research laboratories to the factory floor 'in the near future', according to
Joseph Engelberger, the president of Unimation. When he
addressed the 1980 meeting of the American Association for
the Advancement of Science, in San Francisco, Engelberger
said that industrial robots have already achieved an average
reliability of 400 hours' work without fault, and he listed ten
attributes of the coming generation. These include : mobility
(on wheels, of course, they're easier than legs); recognition
of voice commands; rudimentary vision and a finer sense of
touch, so that the robot can assess its surroundings, locate
different objects, and pick them up right way round; the
multi-armed ability to switch objects from hand to hand;
more flexible, general-purpose hands; and microprocessors

allowing the robot to work out its own arm movements, thereby saving energy as well as increasing dexterity (only about five per cent of the energy put into an industrial robot is effectively used).

More surprisingly, Engelberger said that these robots would be programmed with safety rules, based on the Laws of Robotics, defined long ago by the science fiction writer Isaac Asimov. These rules would prevent the robot from harming people, itself or other equipment. There we hit a hint of the wider future – truly intelligent machines, which we may need to control in more senses than one. But the brief of this particular chapter is industry in today's world, and within that brief, and in the light of Engelberger's list, I can take the robot one probable stage further: down the mine.

Professor Meredith Thring of Queen Mary College, London, has been commissioned by the National Coal Board to 'propose the first steps of an evolutionary approach' to robotic mining. He says the mines could be totally unmanned underground within ten years if the Coal Board 'put their backs into it'. Coal Board officials do not agree. Some of them say it will take twenty to thirty years, others say the miner will always be needed for repair work.

Thring designed his first robot miner in the 1960s. The 'telechiric' methods he is working on – now, of course, chip-based – involve robots with television cameras as their heads. They would be controlled from the surface by people wearing helmets linked to those cameras. The human controller, checking a piece of underground machinery, could then scan the scene simply by moving his own head to direct the surrogate head. He would control the robots' arms similarly. When the trouble had been located, the appropriate specialist would then don the helmet to direct the repair work. Thring hopes that eventually holographic television will provide more truly three-dimensional control of the robots' work.

The economic impetus to develop such remote control might come from the need to exploit the coal deposits under the North Sea. But there are, of course, other ways of automating mining which make a cleaner break with traditional methods. These include underground gasification, chemical separation, microbiotics (using micro-organisms to digest the coal), and hydraulic mining, in which a liquid jet breaks up the coal for it to be pumped to the surface.

Back in the present, the rapid progress being made in some other fields should help the robot in industry. One is pattern-recognizing computers, getting cheaper and better; another is the industrial use of synthetic glues, powerful enough to stick machine tools together.

Human babies learn quickly to recognize shapes, but computers and robots are still a bit clumsy about it. Efficient pattern-recognition programs require a great deal of computer memory and computer time. Although there are many such computers at work, even sorting potatoes on the farm, they tend to be dedicated to one task. A team at Brunel University, at Uxbridge, near London, have devised a pattern-recognizing computer which, they say, is ten times cheaper than orthodox ones and capable of dealing with jobs as varied as reading addresses on envelopes and spotting flaws in biscuits on a production line.

The Brunel team – Professor Igor Aleksander, John Stonham and Bruce Wilkie – have concocted a novel configuration of chip memories to simplify the problems. They say that a £20,000 grant they have received from the Science Research Council will enable them to build a general-purpose pattern-recognizer, needing no separate computer support. It will classify patterns seen by a standard TV camera, and an operator will be able to instruct it simply by pushing a few buttons. In a biscuit factory, the micro-computer would be shown the ideal biscuit and the operator would then press the 'good' button. It would then be shown a distorted one – with the 'bad' button. After that, it's on its own. It could equally well be switched to biscuit-packing inspection with another brief round of button teaching.

On the second front, the British Cabinet's advisers on technology – the Advisory Council for Applied Research and Development – have emphasized in one of their reports the significance of adhesives technology in overcoming many of the problems encountered in using robots in assembly. But they advocated a further possibility, which you might call bio-glue.

The powerful synthetic glues now finding their way into engineering from the more obvious areas of book-binding, packaging and shoe-making, have been used to construct machine tools better than those made by casting and welding. There have been claims of reduced noise and vibration, higher speeds and a forty per cent reduction in costs. But those adhesives are still not as clever as the barnacle and the limpet in tackling what the advisory council's report called 'adverse circumstances', like wet surfaces.

The report admitted that the 'proteinaceous material which is exuded by the organism' (that's what comes of putting civil servants and scientists together) cannot yet be readily synthesized, but there is at least a possibility that sufficiently close analogues could be produced. However, that prompted Professor Stephen Tobias, who leads the adhesives research at Birmingham University, to ask a slightly deflating question: how great is the reliance of the barnacle and the limpet on suction?

But, bio-glue or no bio-glue, the evidence pointing to an acceleration of automation in the 1980s is overwhelming. Some socialist theorists have used this evidence to hail the computer as the eventual destroyer of capitalism. They argue that if information becomes universally and instantly available to all, and if most goods can eventually be mass-produced for next to nothing in robot factories working round the clock, then what will be the point of trying to sell anything any more?

Therefore, before we leave the factory, it is worth recording that that far-flung theory has failed its initial test in Minneapolis, Minnesota. There, in 1979, the inventor Tony Fox, president of Fox Industries, produced a chip-managed multi-purpose machine tool called the Super Shop, which, he claimed (only half-jokingly), could reproduce itself. But when I suggested to him that he was on to a loser, because the Super Shop's cloning ability meant that he would only sell a dozen or so before purchasers had them breeding like rabbits, he pointed to an order book for nearly a thousand before he had begun full production. But the Super Shop is a serious sign of the times. Fox claims that his multi-purpose machine, only sixty-nine inches long and twenty-four inches wide, will do the work of fifteen big, orthodox power tools costing between 16,000 and 20,000 dollars. The compactness and economy brought by microelectronics means that Fox can make that machine for about 1500 dollars.

The Super Shop also serves as a reminder that so far in our tour round the chip we have tended to walk on the sunny side, with only the occasional shadow cast by old jobs destroyed. The time is overdue to peer into the shade.

12. The six deadly dangers

The dangers involved in the industrialized world's total commitment to the computer can be divided into six categories of ascending importance: crime, inefficiency, ignorance, fear, unemployment and totalitarianism. Although, for clarity's sake, I will first discuss them separately, their net effect on the structure of society is produced by the interaction of all six. Further, evidence is beginning to emerge that the total effect is being reinforced by another factor: unforeseen consequences of using computers, where the mismatch between the generalities of human intention and the precision of the machine has subtly distorted those intentions or produced dangerous side-effects on society outside the original thinking.

That may sound like support for the mystical approach to the computer. It is not. It is just an extension of our already apparent failure to grasp and control the complexities of the societies we have created. The trouble is that the computer is intensifying those complexities at an unprecedented speed, though it is, at least, also offering us the opportunity to analyse them better. The mystical bit might arrive when we create machines less dumb than we are.

It may have surprised you that I put computer-related crime at the bottom of the list. It gets a lot of attention in the media; it is, in the code of the news trade, a sexy subject; and stories of complex electronic fiddles strengthen the public phobia about computers. Certainly, the danger is real – and it is a danger that most computer scientists admit they have, as yet, no complete answer to – but it does need to be put into perspective among the more fundamental problems.

There have certainly been 500 major computer-related crimes in the 1970s, probably many more. Some have involved massive sums. In the United States, computer systems, massaged by fiddling programmers, have allowed railway waggons to be stolen by the hundred and 200 million dollars' worth of fuel to be diverted. A leading expert on the computer criminal, Donn Parker, of Stanford Research International in California, has said: 'The computer programmer has more ways to do damage than any ten criminals with a gun. He is potentially the greatest danger to the business community.'

But there is another side to the coin. Firstly, a lot of frauds could be avoided if firms were prepared to spend the money to make their computer systems more secure. Secondly, it tends to be forgotten that a lot of clerical fraud that was underway pre-computer has been discovered and/or stopped by the introduction of computers.

Donn Parker has built an identikit of the computer criminal from an analysis of 375 computer-related crimes in various countries. It shows an average age of twenty-nine and a high level of computing skill. He or she is regarded by the employer as honest, reliable, bright and highly motivated at work. This new breed of criminal considers it highly immoral to harm individuals, but, in meeting the challenge to beat the machine, they are only taking money from the big organization – and that's not stealing. Most computer security specialists – private and police, commercial and academic – agree with that diagnosis. They also tend to agree on two other central points about computer crime:

1. That much of it is still hidden. Theft by tinkering with the system is often not reported to the police because firms fear loss of public confidence. The London police commissioner, Sir David McNee, has called this attitude short-

sighted and amoral. With the threat of publicity, some suc-cessful thieves have even won golden handshakes – plus glowing references to pass on to their next victims.

2. That many firms still refuse, despite the evidence, to spend the extra money that would make their computers more secure. It is the philosophy of the store left wide open to the shoplifter. Some financial systems lack the audit trails that will nose through the computer, acting as elec-tronic detectives; some lack rigorous codes for access to computer terminals, recording use and granting different levels of power to lift or alter information in data bases. But even the most secure system will not give total protection from the dishonest programmer who is empowered to meddle within. All that firms can do (at a cost) is to make it so difficult for him that it is no longer worth the work and the risk.

A survey by the UK National Computing Centre of four-teen computer-related crimes in Britain illustrated the scope there can be for the criminal. People falsified data entered into systems, invented fictitious account records, altered computer programs, rewired communications equipment and created phantom suppliers and customers. The Com-puting Centre reported that the amounts taken ranged from fifty pence to millions of pounds, with the majority of cases in the £10,000 to £50,000 range. All the thieves were sacked – but not all were prosecuted. Of those who were con-victed, most were made to pay back the money and given suspended sentences. Only a few were gaoled; their sen-tences ranged from four months to four years.

This matches the US experience, that courts tend to let off lightly these 'respectable middle-class' criminals. Pros-ecutors also face the problem of presenting evidence about computer programming in terms that juries will grasp. Although many of these crimes are straightforward – taking the opportunities presented by a wide-open system – others involve subtle techniques. For instance, there is what Donn

Parker calls the salami technique – changing programs so that a minute sum (say one cent in a thousand dollars) is sliced from hundreds of accounts and constantly credited to the thief's account. The sums are so small that the customer-victim rarely notices and doesn't bother if he does.

Then there is the trapdoor technique, whereby someone with the knowledge and time to study a system can take a programming route to its heart, making elaborate entry codes irrelevant. But perhaps the most perilous is the Trojan Horse. Once someone with a grudge has mastered the system, he or she can insert a dormant instruction – the computer will then go bananas X months later.

This portfolio of dangers is causing increasing concern among computer manufacturers. Carl Hammer, director of computer sciences for Sperry-Univac in Washington, has given a series of lectures on the problems. He is an apparently mild and liberal-minded man, now into his sixties, but his recipe for computer security verges on the totalitarian: when you apply for a job in a computer installation you submit to 'a thorough background investigation'; when you start the job you wear an identity disc that will be checked by the security guards who patrol day and night – especially night; and if you break the security rules, you are fired on the spot and marched straight out – so that you cannot get your fingers near a computer keyboard.

Hammer is frank about the failings of the computer profession. Security practices are 'often inconsistent, to say the least'; managers and supervisors bypass established procedures; computer operators do not fully understand the multiple complexity of the risks; in addition, 'current computer operating systems – especially for large machines – are plagued with software problems for which there seem to be few, if any, remedies.'

This brings us to the second danger on our list: inefficiency. Hammer estimates that fifty per cent of damage or loss in computer systems is caused by human error and omission; fraud and theft account for perhaps fifteen per cent; malicious damage fifteen per cent; and natural hazards, like fire and flood, twenty per cent. He says: 'The problem with our current society, in the post-industrial environment, is its complexity. In order to govern ourselves, we need to collect more detailed data than ever.' The result, as we have seen, is bigger and more complicated computer systems – and many of them are made even more vulnerable because, through the development of computer networks with remote terminals, they become shared resources. Even listing all the vulnerable components in a computer network has become a major task; and the speed of development means that the list of compound possibilities needs constant updating. It may be decades, Hammer believes, before the maturity of software design matches that of the hardware.

What he is really saying there is that it may be decades before we really control the computers we rely on. Which leads into the next danger: ignorance. But let's linger with inefficiency for a while. Auditors are becoming worried too.

Graeme Ward, president of the UK Institute of Internal Auditors, says that many organizations use computer systems that have an alarmingly low standard of inherent control. His institute is not concerned about computer crime but about the 'fact that many organizations are using the wrong computers to process the wrong data in the wrong way.' All the information available to the institute – 'whose sources are invariably reliable' – suggests that fraud is not a material problem. Computer systems are safer from fraud, Ward says, than manual or partly mechanized systems. But pressure has to be put on computer companies to provide systems and software which are inherently controllable and which can be independently certified as being secure. Ward accuses computer suppliers of irresponsibility in selling machines for which essential software has not been developed.

Ward also criticizes his own people. He says that auditors remain complacent about coming to terms with the computer and are therefore in danger of becoming deaf, dumb and blind in their dealings with computer systems. He blames the low level of understanding of computers partly on the pace of change and partly on the British education system, which has failed to equip the new generations of managers with the basic principles of computing.

The educational problem is world-wide, though many countries are tackling it quickly. (As random examples, Harvard now insists on basic understanding of the computer as one of its entry requirements and many American high schools have replaced typing courses with word-processing courses.) The failure of schools and universities (particularly in Britain) to adapt quickly enough to changing requirements has contributed to the inefficiency of some commercial computer systems. Though, of course, computer companies themselves must take a share of the blame for not investing enough in training programmes.

People blame the mysterious machine when they receive a domestic gas bill for £1 million. Nine times out of ten the machine is innocent. The computer is infinitely literal-minded. It cannot (yet) reason for itself – it has to rely on the human programmer to guide it. As the everyday uses of the computer become more complex, so we require richer analytical talents to ensure that we have precisely translated our intentions into computer language – and also covered all the odd eventualities that could arise in the computer's work and which could direct it down an overlooked bizarre alley, like sending out that £1 million gas bill. Those problems come in two stages: the operating systems that Carl Hammer was talking about, which tell the computer how to organize its own resources, and the application programs (telling it how to do a particular job).

Faults do occur, of course, in the hardware – the machinery of the computer itself – but more often than not it is the human element that fails, often through inaccurate information being entered into systems which do not include programming precautions to protect against such keyboard errors by operators.

The most frightening examples of the ways in which human frailty can be overlooked, when we put our trust in the machine, have happened in the defence sphere. At least twice the United States has approached the borders of nuclear action – first, in 1958, because a missile-detecting computer was said not to have been told that the moon was a missile of a different ilk and, twenty-one years later, through a test simulation of nuclear attack getting into the system proper. Here is a collection of more modest examples, culled from the research of the UK National Computing Centre:

A county court refused to hear any more claims for rent arrears brought by a local housing authority, because, dozens of times, computer statements about the sums owed by tenants had proved to be inaccurate.

When three people died in a thirty-four-car pile-up in motorway fog, an inquest decided that a contributory factor was the failure of the computer-controlled signalling system to change the speed signs from fifty to twenty miles an hour.

A system design error caused a university computer to issue graduates with incorrect degree certificates over a period of two years.

An appeal court cut a drunken-driving gaol sentence after hearing that a computer error had caused magistrates to be told that the driver had a previous conviction for theft at a time when he was abroad.

The failure of a computer system for recording life-insurance policies – a failure which cost the insurance firm about £600,000 – was blamed on a lack of well-defined office procedures. The company explained that it had no experience of computers – and the computer company chosen to supply the system had no experience of life insurance.

The most notorious British example of muddle in transferring a complex clerical operation on to the computer is the national Vehicle Licensing Centre. The stories here include the issuing of full driving licences to provisional-licence applicants and delays of months in licence renewals. One driver submitted six log books to the centre and was sent documents showing that he now owned six Vespa scooters instead of six vintage Douglas motor-cycles.

Carl Hammer's estimate that fifty per cent of computer failures are caused by such human inadequacy is typical of the computer community's corporate assumption of guilt. Mayer Wantman, a director of the training company Infotech International, says that programming errors are still so commonplace that about forty per cent of the average programmer's time is spent in fixing programs rather than creating new ones (debugging, they call it). It can often cost more to write a single program instruction, he claims, than buying the computer itself. He dismisses most programming as 'a mixture of tried method, rule of thumb, and intuition'.

Even more frighteningly, workaday systems analysts and programmers, without the remotest hint of an axe to grind, show the same disillusionment. When one in a group starts talking in visionary terms, there is usually another to say either that it is pointless to talk like that 'when we can't even get the ordinary payroll system right', or to retell the story of the programmer who fled the airport when he heard that the air traffic control system was now computerized.

The British Computer Society, a conservative professional body, not given to embroidery, has issued a report attacking all sides. It said firms were 'disenchanted' with their computer specialists and that the performance of computer systems was often disappointing, because of lack of liaison between users and systems analysts; it accused computer manufacturers of imposing restrictive contracts and forcing expensive and disruptive changes on customers just to suit marketing strategy; and it demanded tougher action to enforce standardization so that companies were no longer 'locked in' to one supplier.

Such concern can no longer be dismissed as a minor industry squabble. The skills and attitudes involved affect our daily lives today and will do so increasingly in the 1980s. The manpower problem is, of course, composed as much of quantity as quality. John Imlay, the 1979 president of the American Association of Software Companies, says that the shortage of computer skills will reach crisis proportions in Europe and the United States in the early 1980s, unless computer-users stop duplicating development effort. The cost of computers is falling so rapidly that 'thousands of new computer users are flooding on to the market each month, all requiring staff.'

Imlay's solution is for companies to buy software packages for their ledger or payroll systems, instead of wasting rare skills in developing their own individual ways of doing things. That's not just wasteful but downright irresponsible, he says. The fact that Imlay's own company sells such packages does not becloud the argument; the concern is echoed on all sides.

The Control Data Institute has estimated Britain's shortage of software people at 20,000, with demand rising by fifteen per cent a year; and that does not include new computer installations, let alone the greater demands on computer expertise developing in engineering and manufacture through the opportunities offered by the chip. In that sector the National Economic Development Council estimates that unfilled vacancies amount to thirty per cent of total need.

Those shortages are creating a bonanza for some. The technical magazines are crowded with advertisements for vacancies in commercial computing, the pay offered seems to rise every month, and the transfer market thrives. One small computer company has offered its staff £1000 worth of holiday vouchers or a video recorder just for introducing a project manager or a technical salesman.

So there is a typical paradox of human society: that as the computer takes over more areas of employment, the computer community itself becomes increasingly short of the skilled manpower needed to keep things moving. It's a world-wide and industry-wide shortage – from the chip-making industry itself (as we saw in Chapter 4), to the companies making computers, the companies using computers, the companies serving the companies using computers, and, recently added to the list, many more companies now wanting to use computers, either routinely in small business or complicatedly in automated manufacture and new products.

There is also a touch of the might-have-been that goes beyond the obvious short-sightedness. According to a team of people who should know, a vein of young talent has been lying untapped for years. It is hidden among school-leavers who have missed the academic boat and who end up in boring, futureless jobs – or with no jobs at all. That is the reasoning behind the National Computing Centre's Threshold training scheme and the centre has evidence to support it. Threshold has produced computer programmers from sixteen-year-olds armed only with the basic British educational qualification, the Certificate of Secondary Education, or even with no paper qualifications. Threshold graduates who are now well-paid programmers include former hotel porters, petrol-pump attendants, and sewing machinists (all jobs being destroyed by the chip, you note). Three years' experience of Threshold has convinced George Penney, the Centre's career projects manager, that about thirty per cent of Comprehensive school-leavers have the intellectual ability to become programmers and that a qualification in English language is a better grounding for a programmer than mathematics. The Threshold scheme relies on the concept of 'programming aptitude' that, in addition to general intelligence, there is a particular flair required for the job of manipulating computers. At one time, Penney says, there was a notion that only graduates could program. But studies comparing test results with the performance of people already employed show a correlation between ranking for programming ability and both spatial ability and clerical accuracy. That seems to place the programmer between the engineer and the clerk. But at the next stage – the systems analyst who draws up the grand design – an additional quality is needed: critical thinking. Penney argues that there are good reasons for regarding analysts and programmers as coming from different populations.

Penney does not agree that the bungles that occur in computer programming are due to the shortage of people or to a lack of quality in recruits. He puts all the blame on inadequate training. Too many people, he believes, go through short courses run by computer manufacturers, which just cover the surface and are not bedded in the principles of programming. He also complains that user-companies are still not willing to invest in training people; they prefer to pay more for trained staff in the constricted market place. He, too, sees an immediate solution in software packages. He believes software houses will concoct more flexible ones to meet the demand as firms increasingly find their programming costs still rising while the cost of the actual computers keeps falling.

Another hopeful sign lies in the generation gap. There is a host of anecdotes from around the world of children teaching their teachers about computers, and there are now often more applications for university computer courses than there are places. My favourite illustration of the generation gap comes from the Design Centre in London.

As part of an exhibition on airports, they had a computer answering visitors' questions. Design Council staff, surreptitiously watching people approach the machine, came to a

145

conclusion which is, by now, folk wisdom: adults tended to fall for the computer's mystique and seemed awesomely impressed that they could have a meaningful relationship with it, while the children understood that they were talking to a mere machine, which relied on the skills of a human programmer, and they tried to defeat the system with their questions. The difference was that the program's deviser – Brian Smith, research fellow in computing at the Royal College of Art – was ready for them.

The routine part of the computer's work was to respond to key phrases from questioners – like 'luggage delays' or 'checking in' – and to supply the relevant information, courtesy of the British Airports Authority. The computer would keep the conversation going by sometimes answering a question with a prompting question or, through storing each conversation, going back to square one – 'Is that what you meant about flight delays?' But Smith anticipated that computer-conscious youngsters would not fall for that, so he prepared a defence in depth.

If the computer was told to '– off', it replied, 'And you too', simply by responding to the word 'off' as a sentence ending. If the aggro continued, the computer had forty-five different – and more conciliatory – responses up its sleeve. If told that it was stupid, it descended to basic sarcasm: 'Thank you very much.' But if told it was talking bullshit, it said, 'Sorry, I'm only a computer.' Smith has taken that idea horrendously further in a program called Abuse (not allowed in the Design Centre), which gets 'more and more hysterically nasty'. It could give a new meaning to the buzz phrase 'man-machine interaction'.

That phrase is no joke. It is computer science's term for the research aimed at removing public fear of the computer. A striking example of the value of this work emerged in 1977 from the man-machine interaction group at the National Physical Laboratory. That group, headed by Chris Evans, a psychologist and computer scientist (who died, tragically young, two years later), produced a micro-computer system aimed at taking some of the workload from the doctor by getting the computer to establish the patient's basic symptoms.

Hospital and surgery trials have supported Evans's passionate belief that once people are in contact with the computer, they love it, not fear it. More than fifty per cent of patients in the first trial said spontaneously that they preferred it to the traditional interview with the doctor. A lot of research went into wording the questions, so that, as Evans put it, patients have 'the sense of a presence, a rudimentary personality' at the other end. The result is that there appears to be no 'social or intellectual barrier' with the machine as there may be with the doctor, nor any feeling of embarrassment. One patient admitted a fifty per cent higher alcohol intake to the computer than to a consultant psychiatrist.

The questions are presented to the patient on a computer terminal, which may be either a TV screen or a tele-typewriter. The patient presses a button to indicate 'yes', 'no', 'don't know', or 'don't understand'. The computer picks the next appropriate question from its store on the basis of the previous answer, and at the end of the interview, prints a summary for the doctor. The sequence is introduced to the patient with a strictly non-patronizing explanation, but in the first trials, if people pressed the 'don't understand' button, they got this simpler instruction:

Hello ... We are trying to find out if computers can help doctors in their work. You can help us by taking part in this interview. If you agree to, then press the button 'yes'. If you would rather not, then press the 'no' button. Go ahead and press a button ... Good. Thank you very much. I hope you'll find it interesting. This is a computer talking to you ...

The problems of fear, the problems of inadequate skills and insufficient trained people, are problems we can at least understand, even if we cannot solve them. But there are indications that the computer has begun to set us problems beyond our comprehension.

These start at the mundane level of everyday business. A number of studies have shown that the failure to achieve clarity between the people building a computer system and the people who will use it can go one stage beyond the obvious, producing a situation in which managers have increasing difficulty in fully understanding the computer operations on which they rely. A Fabian report by two computer academics, Tom Crowe and John Hywel Jones, put it well: 'The computer will do what you tell it to do, but that may be different from what you intended.'

Further, Professor Donald Michie, of Edinburgh University, believes that systems are emerging which not only outrun the intellectual reach of the people using them but do so in a way which is opaque to human attempts to follow what they are doing. That he calls the 'next crisis but one'. He says that computing technology sets no premium on representing information in conceptualized form, though the human brain is entirely orientated towards conceptual representations.

Michie quotes examples in automation and air traffic control where operators have been unable to judge when to step in and take over from the computer – because the machine might have been doing the right thing, but in ways they could not understand. Therefore, we should not go deeper into such areas of computer control, he believes, till more work has been done on instructing computers in such a way that they can explain themselves to their users.

There are indications that something even more disturbing could be happening on the societal scale. We still lack understanding of how the combined effects of different uses of the computer are changing society in unforeseen ways, although the process has been underway for two decades.

One of the difficulties even in assessing, let alone tackling, such problems is that most Western democracies rely on outmoded mechanisms fashioned in a pre-computer world. A senior British government official, closely concerned with policy-making on technology, has admitted that the computer is advancing so fast that it is completely out of phase with society and its institutions – 'certainly within government'.

One of the few detailed studies in this field has been made for the International Institute of Communications by Anthony Smith, a TV producer turned media analyst, and he chose the area of probably greatest significance outside government itself – the consequences of the total computerization of the American press within a decade. In his 25,000-word report he says that the process is accentuating divisions in society and strengthening the position of small elites. Smith's case for drawing wide conclusions from newspapers alone rests on three main points: that computer storage of information is expected to make the greatest contribution of the late twentieth-century to the evolution of human knowledge and consciousness'; that in this technological 'jungle of choice', the newspaper has become a testing ground of something wholly new in human communications; and that, therefore, the American newspaper industry offers an instant laboratory for students of the impact of the computer on society.

Smith describes how the computer has saved the American newspaper (by the methods outlined in Chapter 9), but his particular concern is with the way in which these methods have enabled the metropolitan paper to cope with the death of the inner cities by aiming at readers in the rich, distant suburbs, through electronic transmission to satellite printing plants, and the greater ease the computer has brought to the production of special area editions and area advertising.

He claims that the very efficiency that the computer supplies is dehumanizing newspapers. Because of the ease of using pre-processed information from central sources (like syndicated services), the newspaper is changing from a medium written by individuals for general audiences into a specialized service in which an amalgam of semi-anonymous information is provided for individualized audiences – a suburb of stockbrokers here, a suburb of television executives there.

But the functions of the press as a fourth estate in a democracy demand, he says, that the newspaper is a 'complete social presence; not just a channel for someone else's information'. Newspapers are being locked into patterns of advertising and distribution which make large quantities of information available to small elites. 'Those sections of the audience which do not demand to be informed (and who, in practice, perhaps never were) are now much more completely cut off.'

A distinction that Smith seems to have been unable to draw is between changes that are occurring through totally unforeseen consequences of the computer and those that might have been deliberate uses of the computer to produce financial advantages but societal disadvantages. And, in any case, there is another side to the argument.

While the printing presses still exist, cheaper computer printing has been a factor in the emergence of small community news sheets and more extensive literature from local societies. These have helped to diminish social barriers. And when (or if) the printing press is finally replaced by a multiplicity of sources available on home viewdata-style computers, the small organization, or even the individual, could have an easier access to the widest public. (It might just be significant that British research by the Consumers' Association has found most initial interest in viewdata down market – the Association says that the middle classes in Britain 'are tighter-fisted and more likely to regard viewdata as a gimmicky luxury'.)

Smith does not appear to have considered these possibilities in concluding that mass society is being prepared for important and perhaps undesirable, internal partitions'. But he does add: 'The new technology itself does not change social formation. It merely brings home to us some of the unpalatable truths about the kind of social dividing lines we already have.'

In other words, the computer can clarify as well as affect human behaviour – another aspect of the hoary but sound adage: don't blame the computer, blame the people. Nowhere is that clearer than in the inconclusive debate about the chip and employment.

13. Change without choice

If we are not prepared to change – and change again – then we must be prepared to be materially poor. Granted that there is no remote chance of an international agreement to regulate the pace of change, then, in a competitive world, microelectronics will force us in the 1980s and 1990s to switch jobs and learn new skills several times in our working lives – if, that is, we still want a world of washing machines, deep freezers and Mediterranean holidays.

That (as I indicated in Chapter 1) is the solitary piece of general agreement produced by the obsessive public debate about the chip and employment, which began in Britain in 1977 and quickly spread throughout Western Europe and beyond. Even Japan is now getting itchy and only the United States, of the wealthy nations, seems to be handling the situation coolly, through its tradition of greater mobility of labour. Even with the recent diminution of entrepreneurial faith there, this comment by an American businessman seems fairly typical: 'I can't understand what the European fuss is about. The computer on one cheap chip of silicon is just another chance, another opportunity . . .'

The base of that one piece of agreement in Europe is impressively broad: politicians of left, right, and middle, industrialists, union leaders and academics, all accept that we need to use the chip, widely and quickly. But beyond that, all is confusion, particularly on the central question as to whether microelectronics will create more jobs than it destroys.

In Britain – where organizing conferences on microelectronics was the biggest growth industry of the late 1970s – the debate quickly polarized into a pattern that has become common elsewhere. The orthodox argument – that this technology will create more but different jobs, as all technological advances have done so far – comes from industrialists and economists and from most politicians, of left and right.

The heterodox version tends to come from those few politicians, union leaders and academics who are versed in the technology itself and who take their evidence from current changes. They say that the machine can now replace such wide areas of work that there will be massive unemployment and unrest in the 1980s – assuming that we are indeed wedded to the work ethic. They therefore talk hopefully of an ordered progression to a Leisure Society in which machine-created wealth is used to expand education, health, leisure and social services.

The surveys that have made a disciplined analysis of the prospects – on the basis of aligning the progress of the technology itself with the historical lessons of the speed of change wrought by less ubiquitous technologies – range in their conclusions from a *net* gain of a million jobs in the United States and Western Europe by 1987 to a net loss of more than ten times that amount. But before we get involved in the inconclusive battle of the figures, let's look at the point on which almost all agree: that job security is a relic of the past.

The *Harvard Business Review* has compiled a league table of the probable financial winners and losers in the medium term. Here are its main contents, with explanations added in brackets:

The winners: Financial institutions (more fee-based consumer and business services); electronics, computing, and communications utilities (obvious); the bigger universities (programmed education); insurance (lower life, health, and property claims); big retailers (electronic promotion techniques); minority entertainers (no more domination by big TV networks); speciality retailers (wider reach at lower cost).

The losers: Airlines (less need for business travel); the oil and motor industries (less commuting and shopping travel); TV networks (see above); the paper industry (no more office letters and fewer printed publications); postal services (electronic mail); the construction industry (fewer offices, simpler peopleless factories); general retailers (shopping from home); wholesalers (bypassed).

Those lists do not, of course, necessarily equate with employment. We have already seen that telecommunications is expanding while cutting jobs. The Barron-Curnow study for the British government's Department of Industry included a corresponding list of the jobs most at risk:

Accountants, financial advisors, and administrators (computers taking over wide areas of basic information analysis); draughtsmen (computer design systems); computer programmers (automating the mechanical aspects of the job, leaving only the pure thinking); and more obviously – postmen, telegraph operators, printers, proof readers, library assistants, secretaries, clerks, keypunchers, cashiers, meter readers, TV and phone repairmen (self-healing systems), light electricians, machinists, mechanics, inspectors, assemblers, operatives, materials handlers, and warehousemen.

The brutal meaning of such a list for those with outmoded skills is illustrated by the semi-conductor industry itself. Many nations have now followed the example set by Japan and invested public funds in microelectronics – from Canada, France, Germany and Italy to Nigeria and pre-revolution Iran – and, in Britain's case, that investment has included the launching of a State-backed company to make mass-market general-purpose chips. (Previously, Britain's small indigenous semi-conductor industry had confined itself to making chips designed for specific industries or particular specialist jobs.)

Labour politicians boasted that that enterprise (a company called Inmos, which has continued under a Conservative government) would create 4000 jobs in areas of high unemployment; and local authorities in those areas began to compete to win the factories of this 'new' industry. But when they started to study the requirements, they received a series of shocks.

First, they found that the promise of 4000 jobs was not that simple. Nearly half of those jobs were for scarce, highly paid microelectronics engineers, most of them university graduates. Second, they found that what production jobs there were gave no hope for redundant shipyard workers or foundrymen; the demand was for nimble-fingered young women. Third, they realized that even those few production jobs would disappear within a few years through automation of chip manufacture. Fourth, they learned that a Victorian relic of a factory in a run-down inner city would not suit – the semi-conductor people wanted clean air and vibration-free surroundings to protect a delicate process; but, above all, they wanted an environment that would attract those rare engineers, and their ideal industrial landscape was composed of pleasant countryside, good private schools, high-quality housing, golf courses, and country clubs.

Thus scores of big local authorities in the areas of dying heavy industry got the real message, and an educational process began that was probably of greater value to Britain than all the formal government propaganda campaigns. Those authorities quickly saw the wealth-generating worth of microelectronics and set up joint centres of micro expertise with their local universities, with the aim of encouraging chip-orientated industry to their areas and kicking their established industries into change.

The theoretical basis of that change has been best expounded by one of the new breed of multi-disciplinary academics, Tom Stonier, an American chemist who has evolved into a technologist-cum-social scientist and is professor and chairman of the school of science and society at Bradford University.

In a paper requested by the British government's think tank (but met by them with no enthusiasm), he has forecast that less than ten per cent of the labour force will supply all material needs within thirty years. Stonier stresses that this does not mean that ninety per cent will be unemployed; if we choose the right policies of expanding education, they will be working usefully in the new 'knowledge industries' and in wider health, social and leisure services. He says the labour requirement for material needs could be as low as five per cent or as high as fifteen per cent, but he thinks it is most likely to be in the five to ten per cent range early in the twenty-first century. Like most such forecasts, it is a 'largely intuitive' judgement, rooted not so much in the actual developments in technology as in their projected rate of acceptance.

Among the current examples he gives is the Coal Board's use of semi-automated equipment at the coal face (which we looked at in Chapter 5). This, he says, will cut the labour force by ninety per cent before total automation arrives. (The Coal Board's own estimate is that mining manpower will have been cut by a third for the same output by the turn of the century, before the industry 'turns in strength' to robots or to direct underground conversion of coal to gas or liquid.) Stonier compares the expansion in the uses of the computer with the history of the steam engine. That began as a device to pump water out of mines before becoming a multi-purpose machine. Similarly, the computer began as a mathematical calculator – but it is moving faster than the steam engine did.

In papers presented to a number of conferences, Stonier has used the premise that technology is the primary driving force of social change to build a structure of three industrial revolutions. The first dealt with devices which extended human muscles; the second – the electronic revolution of the mid-twentieth century – dealt with devices which extended the human nervous system (radio, television, phones, films); and the third, the current computer-based information revolution, producing a post-industrial economy, deals with devices which extend the human brain.

The technologically advanced nations are into that third revolution; the socialist camp is likely to enter it late in the 1980s, he says; and the Third World, including China, will do so over the next few decades thereafter. The nineteenth-century transition was from agriculture to manufacturing; the current shift is from manufacturing to services.

Stonier is optimistic about the transnational implications of this, not only in communications but in multinational manufacture, where the various components of aircraft or computers or whatever can have a global history today. His main supporting evidence is the oil crises of the 1970s – 'the first time in history that minor military powers threatened the supply of a strategic resource of major military powers without precipitating military action.' He also supports the orthodox optimism that wider communications will ensure greater democracy.

Where Stonier undoubtedly represents the universal view is in his emphasis that what is happening today is only a progressive escalation of the automation that has operated for centuries: 'At the beginning of the eighteenth century over eighty per cent of the workforce laboured on farms to feed the rest. Today it takes less than three per cent in the United States to feed not only the rest in that country but much of the world as well.'

This restores us from global theories to immediate repercussions. One of the most buoyant conclusions about employment in the 1980s comes from a two-year study by the American management consultants Arthur D. Little. They make the 'conservative' forecast that microelectronics will provide a net increase of at least a million jobs in Britain, France, West Germany and the United States by 1987. The US will take sixty per cent of those and the split of the European share will depend on how quickly and extensively each country responds to the challenge of ditching the old and embracing the new.

The study, sponsored by sixty clients, including several governments, looked at the microelectronics market in the four sectors that are expected to undergo the greatest changes – cars, consumer goods, business communications, and manufacturing and process industries. It concluded that the market for products containing silicon chips will reach at least £15 billions by 1987 in the US and Western Europe. That will mean 800,000 additional jobs in the four sectors surveyed – jobs derived directly from the end products, not counting the extra employment in ancillary services. The report forecasts particularly fierce competition in the business communications area, but the biggest growth will be, it says, in consumer products – from programmable video recorders down to musical door-chimes.

But the project director, Jerry Wasserman, is unwilling to commit himself on how many old jobs will die to create that overall net increase of a million. He says that the potential of 'intelligent electronics' is endless but that the surge of new jobs will require new skills and there will be at least temporary 'employee dislocation'. Some older people who cannot adjust to change might become unemployable.

This bullish view is supported by a survey made by the UK Department of Employment. It says it found no evidence of microelectronics destroying jobs, though it accepts there has been a loss of job opportunities in some sectors; and it makes the standard point that the economic dangers of a 'dangerously slow' pace of adaptation are far more serious. The British government seized on this report to denounce 'wild predictions' of unemployment which could further slow the pace of adaptation.

Yet those making the 'wild predictions' also accept that rapid change is an economic imperative. The difference is that they say that among the changes required is an abandonment, at least in part, of the system that has served us passably up till now, whereby payment for work is the basic arbiter of wealth.

Thus the Barron-Curnow study, which forecasts that microelectronics will put four or five millions out of work in Britain before 1990, also argues that if people cannot adjust to that, then Britain will become the first de-developed nation. It says the objective of policy should be to make labour displacement acceptable by ensuring that it does not convey social hardship or stigma and by providing the people involved with creative opportunities for the future.

Broadly similar conclusions about employment were reached in France by the Nora report, a document which prompted President Giscard d'Estaing to call for a broad public debate on the computer and society. Simon Nora, the French Inspector General of Finances, said in his report, *L'informatisation de la societé*, that France had to abandon full employment to modernize her industries. He mentioned predictions of a thirty per cent cut in banking and insurance employment through automation in the 1980s.

In Britain, the comforting Establishment view that we can carry on essentially as before seems to contradict itself. The Department of Employment survey, for instance, says that the large-scale use of robots in manufacturing will not arrive until the 1990s and the paperless office is still some way in the future; yet its central gospel is that we must make these changes fast or sink.

The Minister who warned against 'wild predictions' – James Prior, the Employment Secretary – was saying nine months before, when in opposition, that we may have to move away from the work ethic and think of payment for life for not working. He said it was quite wrong to talk of a return to the employment levels of the 1950s and 1960s.

Another Conservative Minister, Peter Walker, put the issue even more vigorously when not in government. He said our attitude to automation verged on the lunatic. 'We should rejoice and create a society in which the machine works twenty-four hours a day ... Uniquely in history, we have the circumstances in which we can create Athens without the slaves.' During the 1980s work might become available only to eighty per cent of the population. The next generation would not be satisfied by guarantees that they could work in factory, mine, or boring office for fifty years of their lives. There was an urgent need, he said, to develop a new approach to employment in which the benefits of technology were used for all, to provide a fuller life.

Those brave words, echoed by only a few politicians and trade union leaders, demonstrate that the work issue is not essentially a party political one (a national basic wage could be organized under any ideology) but a struggle between radicals of many persuasions and the deeper conservative power structures of Western European societies.

This conservatism, of both left and right, often shows itself in a paternalistic response to the logic of the chip. A common attitude is neatly summarized by the chairman of Rank Xerox, Hamish Orr-Ewing. He says that attempts to produce greater wealth through deliberately reducing employment would create a meritocratic elite, and the rest of us, however paid, would have no dignity left. There will always be some people, 'less naturally gifted, who would not be able to use large quantities of spare time.'

The most trenchant opposition to such thinking has come from a British union which, it must be said, would stand a good chance of representing that 'meritocratic elite'. This is the Association of Scientific, Technical and Managerial Staff. Its leader, Clive Jenkins, and research director, Barrie

Sherman, have repeatedly savaged the work ethic, refusing
to believe that the current symptoms of unemployment –
identity loss, vandalism, apathy, then anger – are inherent in
human nature. They are just conditioned responses, reinforced by establishment, which would disappear, they say,
with fair shares of the basic cake and an organized progress
to a prosperous three-day week. But they concede that such
an ordered solution would require at least a decade of
national and international agreement. In immediate terms,
they propose a system of bridging pay for people made
redundant by microelectronics. This pay would continue
until a new job was found and would be provided jointly by
employer and government.

Scandinavia has taken the lead in adjusting labour laws
to meet the new circumstances. Norway has given unions
counter-proposal rights when automation of jobs is proposed and Sweden has gone further by ruling, in effect, that
no microelectronic system affecting jobs can be introduced
without union agreement.

The chip has also had the side effect of stimulating unions
into giving slightly greater attention to their international
groupings – in response to the multinational companies' use
of chip-boosted technologies to switch work among the
continents. An example is the semi-conductor industry's
own use of the cheap labour areas of the Far East for
assembly work. Telecommunications can also be used to
bundle clerical jobs across the world.

The International Metal Workers' Federation, in pro-
posing a world-wide campaign to reduce working hours and
provide a shorter working life, has suggested international
union action to make certain multinational electronics companies the first targets for co-ordinated bargaining. And
FIET, the international federation of clerical and technical
unions – whose head of research, David Cockroft, coined
the choice aphorism, 'To look at microelectronics in terms
of job losses is like viewing the invention of the wheel in

terms of an increase in traffic accidents' – has drawn up guidelines whereby the optimum use of the chip might be achieved with minimum social harm.

One of FIET's key points is that governments should plan expansion in labour-intensive industries to replace jobs destroyed by automation. Thus it supports the French government's Nora report in its idea of reinforcing a division already emerging in industry – a division between highly automated, internationally competing industries and manpower-heavy services for a nation's home consumption only. This idea, which to some extent has been used all along by the Japanese, has been taken a depressing stage further by some senior officials in Britain. Their idea is to keep the civil service deliberately less efficient than it might be in serving the public, just so that it can mop up unemployment in clerical work that should really go to the computer.

The international union reports have tended to bring out more sharply than national ones the effects of the computer on work itself. The FIET guidelines illustrate the way in which skill and interest can be removed from middle-range jobs, and a report from the European Trade Union Institute (the research and educational arm of the European Trade Union Confederation) points to a polarization of work between semi-skilled people on the one hand and highly skilled technical staff on the other, with the squeeze being put on skilled manual employment, through the computer reducing maintenance, assembly, and tool-setting work.

A common fear is the Big Brother watch that the computer can provide on a typist's or production worker's output. Word-processors or supermarket checkouts can easily supply individual work rates and there are microcomputer systems which, placed along a production line, can display to management and workers what they have achieved, what they should have achieved in target rates, and their percentage efficiency – minute by minute.

A less debatable source of union concern is the effect on health of working for long spells at computer display screens. Here we have an example of the computer forcing on our attention a problem we have shrugged aside before.

Apparently, for years, nearly a third of the working population have had uncorrected, or inadequately corrected, sight defects. Now long hours spent reading from display screens have brought the problem to notice through a rash of office headaches. The British Business Equipment Trade Association has joined the unions in emphasizing the need for regular eye tests. There was also an early scare about the danger of radiation from screens, but most unions now accept that this is not a problem – provided equipment is well maintained.

However, as we saw in the previous chapter, the most immediate employment problem presented by the chip is the fact that we have barely enough skilled people to keep our present computer-dependant world running. This problem goes far beyond those skills directly related to the computer. One of the most powerful restraints on change in industry today is the shortage of engineers to design and produce the mechanical parts and the sensory instruments of automation. That is a particularly British problem, born of an educational system that turned its back on the practical world in Victorian times. An equally urgent problem, and one less peculiarly British, is to alter general education to prepare the next two generations for a post-industrial world.

In 1978, the British government set the educational establishment the task of changing the school curricula to take account of the alterations that microelectronics will bring to domestic and working lives and to ensure that within five years the shortage of trained people is not a constraint on exploiting the technology. Two years later there was little sign of either aim being remotely achieved.

University vice-chancellors and school heads alike have said that the 'lead time' for a fundamental change in teacher training to reach the classroom is forty to fifty years in Britain, though the Department of Education says this is an exaggeration. The reasons for such extraordinary estimates of delay are the over-devolved structure of British education and the cloistered traditions of teaching. Sir Ieuan Maddock, secretary of the British Association for the Advancement of Science, in emphasizing that change needs to reach the primary schools, says that many headmasters are not just indifferent to technology but positively hostile.

Examples of junior school children tinkering with computers are so rare in Britain that the few outcrops are the subject of television news items. The Schools Council has made a rough estimate – rough because no one really knows in a decentralized education system – that only twenty per cent of Britain's secondary schools have a computer and most of those cannot afford more than one microcomputer. In contrast, France is installing 10,000 microcomputers in the schools, both as general teaching aids and to give children computer literacy.

A report by Stanford Research International (an offshoot of Stanford University in Silicon Valley) has pointed out that as information may become the key to wealth and power in the future, so there are likely to be the 'information rich' and the 'information poor'. Recent tests in the United States have shown that many adults are functionally illiterate, unable to read a bank statement or fill a tax form. SRI says : 'The new technology will place greater demands on people's skills. At first, the gap may occur along generational lines, as younger people educated in schools where computer literacy is part of the curriculum have an advantage over older people. In the long run, a new kind of class structure may arise, built on the ability to assess and use information.' (The Smith study of the American press, you may remember, made a similar point.)

The Vice-Chancellor of Aston University, John Pope, says that the educational debate has still not faced the brutal realities of the decline in work for the unskilled. Twenty years ago seventy per cent of workers were unskilled; today the percentage is less than fifty; soon it will be less than twenty. If the unskilled are not given the opportunity of developing creativity, he says, vandalism will increase and violent revolution will follow. Yet those who feel that the connection between education and survival – earning a living – should be restored are frowned upon by educational theorists. Abstract learning might be right for the very bright, who have a natural thirst for knowledge, 'but what about the less able, the great majority?' Pope's solution is to develop the creativity that all children have. The separation between the academic and the practical is fatal, he says, and a better response might be obtained within education by giving equal emphasis to using one's hands and eyes.

The Council for Educational Technology, in a report which talked of the 'desperate urgency' of educational change, suggested a set of principles for the new pattern that schools should follow: to help people prepare themselves for a rapidly changing society; to fit themselves for employment in new, technologically advanced, and changing jobs; to fill their (increased) leisure hours; and to maintain their self-esteem when there are no jobs for them.

David Firnberg, for five years director of the National Computing Centre, and one of the employment bogey-dispellers – 'More people are probably employed making pocket calculators than ever made mechanical ones' – says that today's children will grow up in a world in which computing will be all-pervasive but largely invisible. As with the phone and TV, few people will know how computers work, but many people will need to know how to use them. The educational system, therefore, should focus on the applications of computing rather than its science.

Taking that argument further, Professor Stonier says that an education system which is primarily job-orientated is a waste of time in preparing youth for the next century. Stonier has an extreme approach to the increasingly fashionable notion of temporary retirement in middle age, with the young doing the necessary work, instructed by the old. He suggests that once adult education is expanded, the school leaving age should be lowered to fourteen or twelve, allowing any youngster who has a job lined up to leave until he or she is ready to return. Stonier claims that university education today merely turns out more of the semi-educated. 'Neither training in the classics, the arts, the humanities, nor the specialized scientific or engineering disciplines is likely to create decision-makers with the understanding and imagination to devise the research programmes to exploit the potential of vast resources.'

Let's go beyond that to the fringe. Some alternative technology people see the chip as their ally in demonstrating that the mechanisms of Western society are too rusty and rigid to cope with the increasing complexity and speed of change. Therefore, we need to build a more decentralized society, with self-supporting communities based on small, new enterprises – away with bureaucracies and power-hungry party politics.

Such sentiments are moving inwards. Sir Hugh Ford, Pro-Chancellor of the Imperial College of Science and Technology, has wondered aloud whether Britain's reluctance to react with the speed of Japan, the US, and Germany might have some wisdom and be more truly representative of what the post-industrial world is about. By keeping up with the Joneses we might find ourselves regretting the loss of some aspects of our civilized existence. Sir Hugh's alternative is to expand our agriculture sufficiently to meet about three-quarters of our needs and to supply the rest through encouraging those small-business sidestream areas of high technology where the UK is already in front.

The world of Jane Babbage owed a lot to alternative technology – or, at least, intermediate technology. And

166

certainly a more fragmented society, consisting of small communities, created by consensus, yet rooted in world-wide communication, might do a lot to ease the even meatier problems presented in Chapter 14.

14. The threat to privacy

George Orwell didn't guess the half of it. His brilliant and frightening picture of life in 1984, written in the 1940s, vastly underestimated the power of the tools that would become available to a technology-based dictatorship, even by 1974. Although his party members were supervised at home and work by two-way telescreens (which would still be highly expensive to use in mass today), they could at least escape into the anonymity of the slums of the Proles, where only human surveillance was likely to catch them. In the real 1984, the computer could trail them anywhere.

The key word is correlation. Many campaigners for civil liberties say that the computerization of personal records does not bring a change in principle; what matters is the collecting of private information on individuals in any form, whether by government departments or commercial concerns. But once such data is in a computer system, the change in scope is so enormous that points of principle become pedantic. Items previously held on paper, and stuffed into filing cabinets in several different government or company departments, can be correlated into a comprehensive dossier at a speed and to a depth that would have been inconceivable before.

This becomes particularly easy if the country concerned uses a UPI (universal personal identifier) – and several do. Once each citizen has his number, used on every form and record, then correlation becomes faster and more comprehensive. The world of Jane and Joe Babbage depended on the UPI, though in fact Britain has no such system. A government inquiry has recommended that if a UPI were seriously contemplated in Britain, it should not be allowed without specific legislation and not before its privacy implications had been investigated. In 1974 the French government decided to use the national register of the citizenry as the basis of a computerized information system, which could have coordinated criminal, medical, social security, tax and other records, putting together almost every fact known to the authorities about any individual. Public reaction to this idea led to the formation of a commission upon whose recommendations France's data privacy laws are based. In 1977, the United States Privacy Protection Study Commission mentioned the risk of drifting towards a UPI without legislation if a particular identity number came to be widely used.

When Orwell's Winston Smith dared to go shopping in Prole territory, the Thought Police were needed to track him. In a real 1984 one official of the Thought Police could know it all within a minute, by punching a few keys on his computer terminal. If all transactions were electronic, the watcher in a society with no legal constraints on personal information could tell immediately what Winston bought, where and when, how he travelled, whether by car, plane or train, what his doctor thinks of his liver, and what the local police sergeant thinks of his family life.

Attitudes to individual privacy vary widely across the democracies. Sweden was first, in 1973, to enact a law to protect the citizen against the misuse of personal information held in computer systems. The United States followed in 1974, West Germany in 1976 (though there were local laws in Germany before that), and, at the time of writing, ten other Western nations had such legislation – and Britain was still not among them. A public opinion poll in Sweden put the protection of privacy as the third most important public issue, after unemployment and inflation;

but in Britain the London Police Commissioner seems to be justified in his claim that most people are not very concerned about gaining access to personal data about them held in police computers – though those computers have details, however prosaic, on nearly half the adult population.

The British experience provides two advantages. It allows at least a keyhole look at one of the few remaining uncorseted uses of the computer by police forces in a democracy; and it has led to an impressive analysis by a government inquiry which has exploited the experience of other nations where legislation is in operation.

But before we go into that, there is one point of total gloom to make. Just as it is impossible to make a computer system completely impervious to the knowledgeable criminal, so most computer people say that, however many inspectors you employ, it is impossible to ensure that a computer network is not being used to play illegally with personal information. It is like looking for the needle in a haystack where every strand of hay is on the move. A survey conducted by the Institute of Data-Processing Management, which showed that most computer managers believe that the sooner data protection laws are introduced in Britain the better, also showed that sixty-five per cent of them – in nearly 400 companies – believe that legislation will not catch people who deliberately hide what they are doing with their computers. That survey also indicated the extent to which computers do handle personal files – sixty-nine per cent agreed that their companies would be affected by privacy legislation.

However, most of the concern expressed in Britain has not been about commercial misuse of computers but about those computer systems intended to serve the community in police and government departments. Here the police have not helped their own case by refusing to give information to the Data Protection Committee, the government inquiry which took over two years to reach agreement on legislative proposals.

One can draw a distinction between the system about which official information has been given – the Police National Computer, which was falsely said at first to contain only factual information – and those systems about which the police will say nothing, the criminal intelligence systems, which contain opinion and speculation as well as fact.

The Police National Computer at Hendon in North London is the centre of a network of about 300 computer terminals at police stations around the country. The Hendon centre had about £35 millions spent on it in the 1970s. In 1980 its scope was being trebled to enable it to deal with a quarter of a million enquiries a day. Through the police radio networks, officers on patrol, in cars or on foot, can be given information from the national records within half a minute.

The network carries an index of the national criminal records, a file of vehicle owners and stolen and suspect vehicles, a fingerprint index, and a list of missing and wanted people. The criminal records index covers aliases, basic description, and certain 'indicators' such as whether Scotland Yard's Special Branch has an interest in that individual or whether his convictions – if he has any – include violence or the carrying of firearms. It is now acknowledged that the system holds suppositional information of a kind which could include unfounded theories about innocent people.

The Home Office, the government department with overall responsibility for the independently organized area police forces, has said that the Police National Computer has no links with other computer systems in central government or with criminal intelligence systems, and no such links are planned. No local police computer linked to the national computer is, or will be, permitted to be connected directly

171

to a local authority system. But, despite parliamentary assurances to the contrary, evidence has emerged of information being passed between the tax authorities, the vehicle registration centre, and social security offices. Also, 'sensitive' police information is held – uncoded – in some county council computers.

Police forces use such local authority computers when they lack sufficient computer strength themselves to hold all the local information they need. They build a databank in the council system and enter and extract information via the phone line. The method is used for such things as pay and pension records, much as a business might use a computer bureau. But there are cases where the information shuttled to and fro is far from innocuous, and the Home Office has admitted that in only a few of these cases is a coded security system used. The data concerned is 'not necessarily' criminal records but mainly information like firearms certificates.

The Data Protection Committee challenged police evidence that the national system held only factual details. It cited the inclusion of details of a car *believed* to have been involved in a robbery and the facility to cross-link subjects with their known associates. The Home Office told the committee that links between criminal intelligence and criminal information records would be postponed for about ten years while the public debate on privacy proceeded. The committee's verdict on this was that any such marriage could pose a grave threat to the interests of the individual and should only be allowed with the most stringent safeguards.

Scotland Yard was even less forthcoming about its new criminal intelligence computers. Witnesses from the police refused to give the committee any details, other than to say that the system holds information 'about crime, criminals and their associates, and matters relating to national security'; and that it has a multi-searching capacity which would enable the police to relate, say, cars to people on the

172

basis of scant detail. Further information has been unearthed by newspapers – some of it pathetically repeated in the committee's report and none of it denied by Scotland Yard. The system can hold data on about 1·5 million people – many of them people without criminal records. It contains 1·23 million files of the Special Branch, 29,000 files from the national immigration intelligence unit, 160,000 from the national drugs intelligence unit, and 67,400 from the Fraud Squad. The police have confirmed those categories, though not the figures.

The extent to which this can go if there are no legal checks was shown by the discovery of the ways in which the police vetted jurors for an Old Bailey trial in 1979. They obtained – presumably from the computers – data on people whose family or friends have records; people who live in squats; who complain about the police; who have children the police have charged but failed to convict; who have expired convictions under the Rehabilitation of Offenders Act; and people who have been the victims of crime. One woman was listed as associating with a criminal, although other entries indicated that he had not necessarily been convicted of any crime.

That sort of evidence demolishes the argument that the innocent have no need to fear police use of computers. There are doubts about accuracy as well. There is a story, which the Home Office has not denied, that while she was shopping, the wife of a policeman heard someone say that Mr A 'fancies little boys'. Her husband entered this 'intelligence' into an experimental criminal intelligence system being run by the Thames Valley police. Two American visitors to the computer installation were handed a computer printout which related the titbit about Mr A. Senior police officers were said to be horrified when told. They had the rumour taken out of the system, then found that there was not the remotest foundation for it anyway.

The Data Protection Committee's conclusion about Scotland Yard's intelligence system was harsh: 'Our Metropolitan Police witnesses clearly regarded this computer as falling outside our terms of reference. However, mention of a multi-factor searching capacity ... leads us to infer that this is a full-text retrieval system. If that is so, it introduces a new dimension of unease ... While we have no reason to believe that the public need be unduly alarmed by the general use of computers for police purposes, in relation to the Metropolitan Police we do not have enough evidence to give a firm assurance to that effect.'

Full-text retrieval means the sort of library-like system outlined in Chapter 5, in which documents are stored verbatim and the searcher finds the document, or collection of documents, he wants by telling the computer to search for a combination of key words. This is ideally suited for surveillance, particularly in such a system's ability to correlate apparently unconnected items of information to supply a significant picture. It could, for instance, compile a list of all National Trust members who own black Minis and have red hair; or all shop stewards who have been known to meet a particular MP and who took a holiday last July.

The Data Protection Committee was told by the Home Office, the Association of Chief Police Officers and the Metropolitan Police that all police computer systems should be exempt from privacy laws. But the police witnesses emphasized that they did not want decisions about how police computers were used to be in their own hands; they wanted this responsibility to lie with the Home Office or with Parliament.

Nevertheless, the committee stuck to their supervisory guns. 'We believe', they said, 'that the best way to avert any fears and suspicions of such systems would be for them to be subject to the legislation which we propose.' But in none of the police areas did the committee recommend that individuals should have the right to inspect information held about them. It is on this fundamental question of 'the right to know' that the British proposals differ from the line adopted by most other Western democracies.

The Data Protection Committee's 460-page report, published in December 1978, and still not acted upon eighteen months later, could serve as a text on the whole question of the impact of the computer on society. It's not only thorough; it's also, for an official document, very readable. But, in the eyes of many, it has fudged the issue by largely rejecting the principle of the right to know.

Much of the legislation now in operation around the Western world gives the individual the opportunity to inspect and, if necessary, correct personal information about him held by governments or companies. The British report says, in effect, that this is too simplistic in view of the many and varied and still growing uses of the computer. It says that a data protection law should be different from a privacy law in providing a balance between public and individual needs. It proposes, therefore, a series of codes of practice – perhaps fifty in all – which would be negotiated with the different computer users of personal information. These codes of practice would be drawn up by a Data Protection Authority, which would have wide powers of inspection and enforcement and would be free of ministerial control.

The authority's work would be governed by seven principles, the crucial one being that people should know 'what personal data relating to them are handled, why those data are needed, how long they will be used, who will use them, and for what purpose.' But the individual would not himself be able to check on this in all areas, and certainly not in the case of police systems. In the medical field, patients would be entitled to check purely factual data on their records but not to see such items as medical diagnosis and prognosis. Clients of the social services would normally be allowed to see social workers' records – which, the committee said, would lead to 'an improvement in the accuracy and quality of the information recorded'. Education and employment records would also be open to inspection, with the possible exception of performance forecasts and career and salary prospects.

All central and local government computer systems – though not necessarily all commercial systems – would have to be registered with the Data Protection Authority. The only exception to this rule would be 'precisely limited' to national security; even there, there would be no exemption from the principle that information collected for one purpose should not be used for another without the consent of the person concerned. So security officials would not be entitled to obtain banking or personnel records.

All police systems – including criminal intelligence systems – would be registered and open to inspection by officials of the authority, and codes of practice would be devised for their operation.

Whether or not the methods of control proposed in the UK would be more effective in practice than the omnibus right-to-know approach, there can be no question that Britain is behind the field in tackling the problem. Data protection legislation has been introduced in Austria, Belgium, Canada, Denmark, France, Germany, Holland, Luxembourg, Norway, Portugal, Spain, Sweden and the United States. These laws, of course, vary in scope and method. Some have been embedded in the constitution. Some cover central government only. Some cover all personal information, whether held in computers or not. Some are run by a supervising authority, others by regulation-cum-inspection agencies. But they all include the citizen's right to know, though often with restrictions in certain areas. Only Britain's proposed legislation would leave this principle to be sorted out in the different codes of practice.

Attempts to coordinate these laws internationally are going slowly through the European bureaucracies. A draft European convention being considered would give the individual the right to amend and correct data in both public and commercial computer systems; would provide remedies

for the individual when information about him is processed
or held in another country; and would prohibit the recording
of data relevant to religion, political or other opinion, racial
origin, or leading to discrimination. The EEC has commissioned a year's research work by the National Computing Centres of Britain, France and West Germany, aimed
at establishing the factual foundation for Europe to coordinate data protection laws. This work is, of course,
crucial to the increasing exchange of information between
nations (the buzz phrase is transborder data flow).

The Data Protection Committee said that if British data
protection legislation was long delayed the UK could become a 'data haven', a refuge for companies wanting to
dodge legal restrictions in other countries. Sweden was the
first country to refuse to allow some computer data to be
transmitted to Britain for this reason. As we have seen
again and again, information can now be sent so quickly
and comparatively cheaply by phone line or satellite that
the location of computers is becoming increasingly irrelevant to the work they do.

This is an area in which the computer has contributed to
the growth in size and power of multinational companies.
One of the simplest cases causing concern to trade unions is
(as we saw in the previous chapter) the transference of data
from one country for processing in another, where computer
and/or clerical staff come cheaper. A more complicated
example is the quick correlation of information internationally. Recently, a car manufacturer, wishing to downgrade
the role of an uneconomic plant, was able in one day to
establish the precise costs of various redundancy possibilities for that plant, by assessing how much would be pay-
able to each individual among thousands on the basis of
their length of work – then, on the same day, to assess the
comparative costs in equipment and manpower changes of
transferring that work to several other plants.

Until now, it has been reasonably clear that in this way

the computer has contributed to centralization in both industry and government. It is now a matter of debate – a debate as inconclusive as the employment one – whether that process is being reversed through distributed processing on microcomputers scattered here and there.

The insensitivity that a centralized bureaucracy can show towards privacy, when seizing the advantages of the computer, is shown at its clearest in the handling of medical records. The British Medical Association has told doctors not to cooperate with the government's Department of Health in a project to computerize health and family details of children from birth, because the plan does not comply with the BMA's privacy principles. The government scheme, thus effectively baulked, is based on antiquated batch-processing in computers already used by the regional health authorities for administrative work. Therefore, it would computerize personal records on the cheap – at the expense of the patient's privacy.

The general practitioner or hospital doctor was asked to fill in a form about his patient – a form over which he had no direct control. Batch-processing means that these forms would be fed to the computer – and the information extracted – by the regional health authority's computer staff. The responsibility for ensuring the patient's privacy would lie with them, not with medical people. The only independent security device was the separation of the medical details from the names and addresses of the individuals involved. Only specially authorized staff could relate the two sets of information.

The BMA are not against the computerization of medical records. They recognize that a well-designed computer system is much more secure than a filing cabinet, and they welcome the advantages it can bring both to the treatment of the individual patient and to national statistical studies. They advocate enthusiastically the sort of computer system that is run by the doctors themselves. One such is a scheme at Exeter, in Devon, which has won the British Computer Society's annual award for the computer development of most benefit to society.

That system handles the health records of doctors in two medical centres and two hospitals. Each doctor has a computer terminal on his desk which he operates himself. Everyone entitled to enter or extract information has a personal code number, which restricts access both ways. Only a doctor can enter medical details that alter the records. A doctor can bar access to personal details about his patients even from his partners in the practice. Nurses can use any of the eighty terminals to get basic medical details, but not the doctor's notes, and receptionists can only get the basic identity details, plus prescriptions. Such a medical databank means that doctors no longer have to leaf through ancient notes, and patients no longer need to re-count symptoms they first explained six months before. That sort of system could clearly be linked into a national network to provide a tighter – and swifter – version of what the Department of Health wants. But it would cost a lot more.

When the BMA took their stand against the government project, Dr Paddy Fisher, chairman of their ethical committee, mentioned some of the Orwellian possibilities. If a child needed treatment after falling and banging his head, this would be recorded by the computer – which would eventually link with the Transport Ministry's computer when the now adult person applied for a driving licence. He could be asked to prove that he did not suffer from epilepsy. 'This is not a far-fetched example,' Fisher said. 'It is the sort of thing that could well happen.' It was also wrong that a woman who had a baby should have details of her medical history, including any abortions, recorded. 'I would warn our profession that the danger of Big Brother is all too real.'

We already accept part of that Orwellian atmosphere as a

routine of everyday life. TV surveillance to detect the thief is common in stores. Rooftop cameras are used increasingly by police forces for crowd control and to watch vulnerable areas like Hatton Garden, the centre of the London diamond trade. Digital editing techniques (Chapter 8) could soon be added, to bring a face in the crowd into instant close-up.

Microelectronics is also a faithful and neutral servant of all sides in the battles of industrial and national espionage. The techniques of bugging have gone beyond the planted pinhole microphone and miniaturized camera to lasers that can pick up a conversation half a mile away by interpreting the vibrations of the window glass in a room.

The growing reliance of companies on information and communication seems to have been matched by an increase in industrial espionage. A senior police computer expert says the extent of industrial spying is difficult to assess because – just as with computer crime itself – firms will not admit they have suffered, since it could affect their share price. One security firm claims to have made security sweeps for over twenty British companies and found phone bugs in three of them, an oil firm and two advertising agencies. And the Post Office (to which UK customers are supposed to apply for permission to use debugging and coding equipment) says that the demand for encoding of data transmitted on computer networks is increasing.

If the electronic criminal can break into a data transmission he can not only get the message but change it as well. Therefore data ciphering systems are getting more complex, with the code keys stored in locked units, with those keys automatically modified at random, and with automatic alarms that block the transmission if anything odd is detected. For the fringes of the networks, microelectronics has made possible pocket-sized units for enciphering and deciphering messages.

One of the simplest safeguards to break is the phone

scrambler. If you cut into a scrambled conversation, it sounds like a British Rail announcement echoing round Victoria – except that you cannot distinguish even the occasional word. But a few weeks' expert work can unscramble it. This can be made more difficult by using more than one scrambling technique and switching them about; combining, say, a time variation with a frequency variation. But if you code the phone conversation instead, then all the intruder gets is crackle, and the firms that create these coding devices claim that the codes could not be broken in a century of computer analysis. Also, once the voice signal is converted into digital form, it can be encrypted without producing a Donald Duck sort of distortion at the receiving end. One of the side bonuses of fibre-optic communications is that they will make life more difficult for the electronic snooper.

There, then, is the evidence that the computer can be used to threaten liberty from two directions : through covert observation and, more importantly, through the perfectly legal collection and correlation of personal information. Sir Norman Lindop, chairman of the Data Protection Committee, summarized his committee's conclusions in this potent sentence: 'We did not fear that Orwell's 1984 was just around the corner, but we did feel that some pretty frightening developments could come about quite quickly and without most people being aware of what was happening.'

15. Chips here and there

We have seen, in chapter after chapter, that the silicon chip is becoming all-pervasive in industry and commerce, the universal machine that can be usefully used to revitalize virtually all other machines, the 1980s equivalent of the nuts and bolts of the first Industrial Revolution.

It would be impossible, therefore, in one book to provide even a bare outline of the variety of employment the microprocessor has found in its first decade of work. But there are four important fields which we have barely touched so far and which must, at least, be dealt with in summary. They are medicine, defence, transport and energy. The computer has for years been central to defence, it is becoming so to medicine, and looks likely to become so in transport and energy.

The media's attention to microelectronics in medicine has tended to concentrate on the spectacular – the possibilities of providing better muscular control for artificial limbs, the implantation of chips to supply an electronic version of hearing for the totally deaf, the compact solution of many instrument problems in monitoring a patient's condition accurately and continually, and the use of electronic scanners to produce cross-section pictures of body or brain.

These developments point to the probability that Dr Joe Babbage will take on his rounds a diagnostic microcomputer to examine his patients. (The sort of remote TV diagnosis available to Joe Babbage is, by the way, already in use : Logan Airport, Boston, has a medical studio linked to a local hospital by closed-circuit TV.)

But what has tended to be overshadowed in the public eye is the way in which the microcomputer helps the disabled, both in providing new aids and making old ones better and cheaper. There is now a variety of microcomputers which enable the blind to read without Braille. One of the simplest employs a small device which, when passed over handwritten or printed material, sends signals to a hand-held box. This box has a finger-sized recess containing a matrix of rods, which form the shape of the letters being read and which the blind can recognize by touch. More ambitious versions use miniature cameras not just to recognize the shape of letters but also to relate the letters to a phonetic rule book, and thus they can read aloud to the blind in a synthetic voice.

The British government's National Physical Laboratory and Loughborough University have made a computer system called Mavis (microprocessor-based audio-visual information system) which enables disabled people to operate a keyboard by using a suck-blow tube, joysticks, or switches. As in so many areas, voice control is now being added. In the home, Mavis can work door locks, adjust central heating, or control the lights. Limbless people can also write letters with it, using the suck-blow tube. This works by having the alphabet and a stock of common words displayed on the lower half of the computer screen. The user sucks to obtain the correct column, then blows to get the right row. A final suck confirms selection. This technique has been taken further to enable the totally paralysed to communicate solely by moving their eyes. Skin contacts are placed above, below, and to either side of the eye and the computer then converts those eye signals into words. The procedure is similar to Mavis's suck-blow tube, and final confirmation of the chosen word, as it appears on the computer screen, is achieved by blinking.

Less obvious but equally real benefits to society are appearing from the use of the chip in transport. This began with variations on the classical information network – improving traffic flow by controlling city traffic lights, helping airport flight handling, organizing railway signalling – and by taking the weight of routine work from the shoulders of the airline pilot and the ship's officer. The impetus to move the microcomputer down to the individual car and lorry has come from the increasing need for fuel economy and the demands for control of the poisonous fumes of the internal combustion engine.

But the use of the microprocessor to improve the efficiency of the cheaper car models, through the control of ignition and fuel timing and throttle and gear selection, has been slower than the forecasts of both the semi-conductor industry and the car manufacturers. The problems of economically mating the delicacy of electronics to the crudity of the internal combustion engine have proved deeper than expected.

In luxury cars the micro has been used in more gimmicky ways to provide the driver with wider dashboard information – digital speedometers, clocks and radio controls, electronic control of air conditioning, calculations of distances left on a particular journey, and warning messages about fuel consumption.

Where cost is not the prime control, spectacular results have been achieved. For instance, microcomputers have been put aboard formula-one racing cars where, of course, they encounter extremes of acceleration, vibration, high temperatures and electrical interference. There they have been used not only to improve engine efficiency but also to monitor (every fifth of a second) the suspension displacement on each wheel, the forward and braking accelerations, the lateral acceleration on corners, the road speed and the chassis roll. After practice laps, when the cars go into the pits, the onboard computer is connected to a printer and the data – in graphs as well as tabular form – is then available to determine, quickly and accurately, what adjustments to make to improve the car's performance on that particular circuit.

The next logical step is onboard computer adjustments during races. And after that: whither the driver? You may remember Earl Joseph's forecast (in Chapter 3) that the driverless, collision-avoiding car could be a practical proposition by 1985, but motor-racing people deny that this will destroy their sport. They say that in racing the driver puts in work that is still virtually impossible to describe mathematically, let alone replace by electronics. Karl Kempf, technical consultant to the Tyrrell team, says: 'When Fangio and Stirling Moss were driving, it was seventy per cent the driver, thirty per cent the car. Now it's fifty-fifty. But there will be no way to replace the man for fifty years.'

In public transport, however, it's a different story. The ultimate reason why underground trains today have drivers' cabins with people sitting in them is psychological. Computer-run driverless trains have been introduced experimentally for urban transport in Japan and the United States, and have gone beyond the experimental at airports with terminals a long way from the departure lounges. Systems designed by Westinghouse, which use automatic trains travelling at thirty miles an hour along concrete roadways, to which they are locked by rubber-tyred guidewheels, are used at Tampa, Seattle, Miami and Atlanta airports and should be in operation at Gatwick Airport, London, in the early 1980s.

In Germany, a microprocessor system which takes over the main-line railway driver's functions – observing signals, controlling speed and responding to radio instructions – was due to be tested on the Hamburg-Bremen line in 1981, but with the driver staying aboard to watch the computers working. That system has triple security: two microcomputers work simultaneously, checking each other's performance, while a third stands by to take over if one of the others fails. The eventual aim is to use computer control for 180 mph trains. The method has been tested extensively on goods trains in German marshalling yards.

West Germany has also been a leader in using the computer to improve bus services. Two dial-a-bus experiments, which give public transport the flexibility of the taxi, have been operating since 1978 – one in Berlin, for the disabled only, and the other, in Hanover, for the general public. The Berlin service of forty small buses is being expanded in steps to provide, by 1981, a hundred buses covering West Berlin and offering door-to-door transport for all the city's 8000 handicapped people. The Berlin buses are called by phone or by advanced booking through the mail. They follow no fixed schedule. The driver is in radio contact with the computer control centre (which is run by disabled people). The computer selects the best bus to go to each call, bills the customer, and produces operational statistics for management use.

The Hanover public service is more complicated. You can call a bus from roadside computer terminals at twenty-two bus stops. The terminal gives you a ticket, which states the fare paid, when the bus will arrive to pick you up, how long your journey will take, where you change if you need to go on to another old-fashioned bus service – and when *that* bus should arrive, and how long *that* journey will take. Messerschmitt, who devised the system, argue that it could be of particular value in suburban and rural areas, where public transport could be rekindled profitably, fulfilling the 'social objective' and the 'economic objective'.

Total computer control in the air is an issue even more emotive than computers driving cars and trains. One British expert – Les Walker, of the engine electronics division of Lucas – forecasts that helicopters piloted by microcomputers could be flying by 1990 or, possibly, 1985. The system Lucas are working on replaces the pilot's controls with a push-button panel. It is based on microprocessor control of the engine – and, of course, a helicopter's engine is, in

essence, its wings as well. Therefore, says Walker, the helicopter is an easier option for total automation than the
winged aircraft. There is less demand on those seat-of-the-
pants judgements of the human, analog kind that are difficult to translate into the digital demands of the computer.

Walker foresees pre-programmed flights and, more immediately, simpler flying by human pushing of the buttons,
so that the business executive could more easily become his
own pilot of a company helicopter. Such an idea shocks the
UK Civil Aviation Authority, who grimly reply that such a
pilot would still be required to do 200 hours of airborne
training to get a licence – and they would not license a
computer, however much airline pilots now rely on them.

Nevertheless, plans are being made for a new European
A310 airbus (due to be flying by March 1982) to carry
microprocessors empowered to disobey the captain. These
silicon chips will be in the wings, controlling the motors
which move the flaps and slats (flaps are on the trailing
edge of the wing and drop to increase lift; slats are on the
leading edge and extend to increase lift).

Each of the microprocessors controlling these movements
will have a back-up chip monitoring it. Both front-line and
reserve have to agree – if they don't, they will tell the captain. Should the flight crew order them to do something
against the rules – like withdrawing slats below a safe air-
speed – they will reject the order and tell the captain why.
But if the crew want deliberately to try the unorthodox in
an emergency, the chips will do as they are told when the
order is repeated.

This automation goes further in military aviation. Fast,
low-level strike aircraft carry computers that respond to
touch. With the lightest of fingertip touches by the pilot
they can act faster on split-second decisions than computers which take orders through buttons or voice commands.
These 'touch mask' devices use infra-red light beams which
crisscross the pilot's main display screen. A finger placed

187

on the screen will intercept two beams at right angles and thus alert the computer. A point on the mask can order an emergency turn: one touch and the computer checks the maximum force that pilot and plane can resist, then operates the controls to produce the tightest possible turn. Such masks can also be used to team with a map display on the screen: if a point on the map is touched, the computer will put the aircraft on course for that new destination.

Microelectronics has brought the pilotless aircraft to reality in frightening fashion: through the cruise missiles that speed low across country, fitting their flight to the contours of the landscape.

Some optimists argue that the military's reliance on computer technology could remove the threat of nuclear war. This argument is based on the use of computer modelling and simulation as an essential component of strategic planning. (Just as in business use of computer modelling, the known facts are fed to the computer which then calculates the effect of adding various contingencies to the equation. By this means a business can assess more accurately what is likely to happen to its sales next year if, say, Value Added Tax is lowered while two new competitors join the contest.) Chris Evans, in his book *The Mighty Micro*, concludes that the United States' decision to withdraw from Vietnam was based on computer predictions of defeat. But, of course, such computer analysis depends on the accuracy and objectivity of the man-provided data on which it is based.

The Barron-Curnow study is more pessimistic. It points out the significance that the huge American lead over the Soviet Union in microelectronics has had for the balance of power and reminds us that the current stage, in which the cheap microprocessor is available in quantity worldwide, could shift that balance. 'It is clearly impossible for the US to control the distribution of components costing only a few dollars, and there can be little doubt that the Russian answer to the cruise missile will use American microprocessors as the control element ... The use of information technology is changing many of the assumptions on which the current balance of power is based, and this must be a destabilizing influence.'

On the energy front at least, there can be no doubts about the way man has employed microelectronics. Using computers to control office and factory environments has saved hugely on power, and microelectronics is also a key to a new source of power: solar energy. For many years computers have been used to run the heating, lighting, air-conditioning and night-time burglar and fire alarms in office blocks. They can be programmed for a year in advance with details about days and hours when the building is in use and the temperatures required. They then learn from their own experience to fine-tune that programming to deal with unseasonable changes in the weather. But – the old story – they were costly till the chip matured. Now they are an economic proposition for smaller buildings – small-town schools, for instance. Micro-run systems, costing between £1000 and £2000, can save up to forty per cent on heating bills.

The semi-conductor industry's involvement in solar energy was mentioned briefly in Chapter 4. The photovoltaic method of harvesting the sun's energy (using silicon cells, like the wafers on which chips are built, to produce direct electric current) is undergoing one of its biggest tests in Phoenix, Arizona, in a solar-energy field spread over twelve acres. There is now serious discussion about placing such huge fields in orbit around the earth.

But the Arizona example indicates what a long research road there is to travel before the oil finally runs out; the 500-kilowatt plant at Phoenix Airport, which is costing £4·5 millions, will provide only part of the power required for the airport's new terminal building.

The Arizona project, one of many similar large-scale trials, has been designed by the microelectronics company

189

Motorola, who have one of their main bases in Phoenix. They have teamed with the state and city authorities in an attempt to win a major share of the US Department of Energy's solar programme. The Department is funding competitive experiments to bring the cost of solar power down to £1 a watt by 1983 and 50 pence a watt by 1990. These targets compare with a 1977 cost of £10 a watt and a 1979 cost of £5. William O'Connor, director of Motorola's solar energy operations, describes the targets as tough but attainable. He estimates that in the oven areas of the southern United States, Australia, and the Middle East, solar energy could meet fifty per cent of requirements – 'if you went hell for leather on current technology.'

The twelve-acre field at Phoenix Airport has 14,250 bowl-like concentrators to catch the light. Each is thirty inches across and eleven inches deep. Sunlight is reflected from the curved bottom surface up to a smaller reflecting surface at the middle and top of the bowl – and from there down to the working heart, the three-inch wafer of silicon, the solar cell. The concentrators are mounted, like an army of search-lights, on seventy-five arrays, and a computer constantly tilts those arrays so that they track the sun throughout the day. Arizona is an ideal test-bed. The Sonoran desert region ranks second in summer heat only to Death Valley, with surface soil temperatures in summer exceeding 150 degrees Fahrenheit.

In exploiting these advantages, Motorola started small. In 1977 they produced an array of forty-eight silicon cells to power a traffic counter across a six-lane highway in Glendale, Arizona. It provided eight watts or more, enough to charge a reserve battery and keep the counters ticking off the cars through the night. The next – and cost-effective – stage was to supply power at small, remote installations, like radio repeater stations on mountain tops. After that, villages: silicon cells were used to provide small generators for Indian villages in the Arizona desert. One of these villages previously had only enough power to keep a water pump going; now nearly forty homes there have electric lights and refrigerators, plus a washing machine or two.

Finally, to round up this round-up chapter, here are a few illustrations of the ubiquity of the silicon chip, of the way in which it is helping to solve old problems and to spark new ideas in totally unconnected areas.

First, music: for five years a small company called Pulse Designs, run by an engineer and his musician son from the family home at Ashtead, in Surrey, sold a metronome driven by old-fashioned transistors. The feedback from customers showed a demand for something more versatile. So the son, William Watson, wrote a computer program to clarify requirements. Then he matched a microprocessor with a quartz crystal oscillator, to maintain perfect pitch, and thus transformed the metronome into a 'universal rehearsal aid'. The battery-run machine thus concocted includes a digital display to indicate normal beat speed; accented first beat in the bar; cross rhythms; three coloured lights with (or without) an audible tick; extra fast speeds for simple or compound time; tempo display; and an ear plug.

The chip is also being used, alarmingly, to make synthetic music. General Instrument Microelectronics have produced a single chip pre-programmed to generate twenty-five short tunes. If you want to program it yourself, there are 251 notes to play with. The company blissfully suggests that the chip should be connected to different bell pushes on each door of our homes. Each member of the family would then have his own door-chime call tune, with other codes for the milkman and the neighbours. The standard pre-programmed tunes – 'selected for their international acceptance' – range from 'Jingle Bells' to 'God Save the Queen'.

Next, the chip underwater – miniaturizing the submarine. The microprocessor has made possible a variety of flying-saucer-shaped, unmanned underwater inspection craft, many of them less than a metre across. They are designed

to work in conditions that would be dicey for the diver –
rough seas or zero visibility. One example is Smartie (submarine remote television inspection equipment) made by
a small British group, Marine Unit. Smartie is propeller-
less; it is driven by an electrical pump. Its battery of
cameras includes high resolution and low-light equipment.
The microcomputer on board interprets signals from the
control console of the human operator above, to change
speed and direction; but, in zero visibility, it can manage
on its own – it assesses information from the craft's magnetic compass and gyro and projects its own navigation
target, which the operator aboard ship can follow on his
video screen.

If Smartie is operating in fast currents, the operator can
maintain its position in the water by pressing a hold button.
The microcomputer will then compensate for the effects
of the current, keeping the craft on station without the
operator's help. The hold system can also be used to keep
a steady course at speed. (That is a micro version of computer systems that have been used for a long time, to keep
oil platforms or supply ships over a given spot on the
ocean bed, where the sea is too deep or too rough for an
anchor. The computer directs side-thrusting propellers to
offset instantly the changing impact of wind and current.)

The chip is also helping the human diver. Mervyn Jack,
a lecturer at Edinburgh University, has designed a microelectronic device to unscramble the speech distortions that
bedevil a deep-sea diver. It opens the prospect of making
communication cables obsolete. The distortions are caused
by the mixture of helium and oxygen that divers have to
breathe. Unscrambling equipment, bigger than a television
set, is needed on the control ship before diver can talk to
diver or to the surface. Jack's unscrambler is only eight
inches, by four inches, by two inches, and runs on a battery.
He is now working on ways of getting all the work done by
a single chip; then the whole thing would go into a match-
box.

Jack's first version maintains a high quality of speech reproduction, but its main significance lies in the use of such a portable decoder to provide the diver with radio. Then, if the lifeline to diver or diving bell were cut, divers could stay in contact and therefore make rescue easier.

Now, one example from among the many of the ways in which the chip revolutionizes the routine tasks of industry: in this case, testing springs. The traditional mechanical method of testing springs is to put a sample into a machine, which compresses it, and then to measure the load on the spring and its deflection by a slow series of gradual compressions, readings from those compressions, then more compressions, then more readings ... A chip-run machine evolved at the Cranfield Institute of Technology does all that and more in a few seconds. The operator tells the microcomputer what he wants to know. The computer instructs a high-pressure hydraulic cylinder, which compresses and relaxes the spring just once; and, from those few seconds, measuring instruments feed a host of readings to the computer.

The chip is also hastening the arrival of computer animation. This combines the drawing-on-the-screen uses of computer-aided design with the graphic capabilities used in business systems to produce diagrams and graphs from raw statistics. Such computer-produced graphics are now beginning to appear in television commercials and in cartoon films – where the computer can take the artist's definition of the funny walk and reproduce it to avoid the expense, tedium and time-wasting of redrawing every step of the character's progress from point A to point B.

Then, of course, there is the wide and growing variety of usually puerile but obsessional computer games – screen tennis, maze puzzles, spacecraft piloting, and the like. These serve purposes beyond the trivial: they make the computer familiar to the uninitiated; they provide a greater commercial impetus for research into voice communication with the computer; and they may also help to bring more attention to the often unheeded problems of designing computer systems with people in mind.

Among the smallest and the cleverest of these are the chess and bridge playing computers, which look like overgrown pocket calculators and which have had voices added to intone the state of play. Their progress beyond the primitive illuminates the long-term concerns of the artificial-intelligence specialists. Let's now make that leap ahead.

16. The living computer

'I think, therefore I am.' ... Computer science is bringing a sharper piquancy to the ancient debate. The alarmist view is that the self-aware computer, using much wider resources than any individual human brain, could be pushing us around before we have even sorted out – philosophy and religion apart – how our minds work.

Some say, parallelling the arguments about genetic engineering, that the deeper aspects of artificial intelligence research are too dangerous to meddle in. For instance, Joseph Weizenbaum, a pioneer in the field and a professor of computer science at Stanford University in California, believes that artificial intelligence research should be curbed right now. In his book *Computer Power and Human Reason*, he discusses the psychological and ethical issues that the subject raises, attacks the 'imperialism of instrumental reason', and warns against the dangers of assuming that we could ever talk of such human concepts as risk, trust, courage or endurance in terms of a machine.

Most academics working in this field are touchy about talking of the self-conscious computer, anyway. Many of them say that the search for it is meaningless. There is no intellectual chasm for the machine to jump; it is a quantitative question, not a qualitative one. A machine sufficiently deeply programmed by human beings and with a sufficient store of information could do better work than us – and stay under our control. To worry whether that machine is aware of its own existence is just to get muddled in semantics.

A simple way of putting that quantitative case is to imagine a computer with the virtually inconceivable capacity of holding all the possible moves in chess. You make a move, the machine then goes through all the possible moves it could make, all the possible responses from you, right to the end of the line. It selects the best option from those multi-trillions of possibilities for its every move. That computer never estimates, never reasons, and only selects with mathematical inevitability. It wins every time. It reduces chess to dust.

To bring that raw argument down to reality, take a present-day computer, infinitely more restricted, yet still with huge resources of fast calculation and storage – but much more subtly programmed. It does not attempt to go through all the options. It does not operate simply as a mammoth calculator. It follows human-set rules of selection, but rules defined, then refined, through a chess master conducting a dialogue with the machine – using the concept of 'knowledge refining', which we discussed in connection with viewdata in Chapter 6. Such a computer program is confidently forecast to beat the world chess champion of 1990 or thereabouts. (Similar boasts have been made since the 1960s and have always failed. The computer scientists' main excuse has been one of cost, and the cost of computer power is, of course, still dropping.)

But that is still only a surface representation of the quantitative case. It is subtler than that. In a number of instances computers have produced 'original thinking', not strictly within the confines of their programming. The most frequently quoted example is the computer analysis which produced its own proof of the theorem which shows that the base angles of an isosceles triangle are equal – the computer simply flipped the triangles through 180 degrees and declared them to be congruent.

There are also examples in robotics research. Robots can solve simple spatial problems by interrupting what their cameras and tactile sensors tell them, and the results of this research are now emerging into the real world of industrial automation, as we have seen. That progress to commercial reality has taken a long while – it is more than a decade since a robot at Stanford University, when told to push a box off a platform, first located a ramp, then pushed the ramp to the platform, then rode up the ramp to tackle the box; and the use in artificial-intelligence research of robots sensitive to their surroundings goes back to the early 1950s – the work at Queen Mary College, London, mentioned in Chapter 3, is a recent example of it.

This approach of teaching the machine to learn – which some say will eventually produce machines that are truly sentient but sentient in ways foreign to humanity – brings us to the multi-disciplinary requirements of artificial-intelligence research. It works both ways: psychologists, physiologists, neurologists, philosophers, mathematicians, engineers are all involved with the computer scientists in advancing artificial intelligence and, at the same time, advancing our own understanding of our mental and physical processes and the machines we use and the ways in which we use them.

Richard Gregory, now professor of neuro-psychology at Bristol University and formerly in Edinburgh University's machine-intelligence team, is looking at the problems from the neural standpoint. He believes the psychologists are getting too hung up about the sub-conscious: few of our neural processes are conscious, anyway.

Take the game of cricket. The ball travels at eighty miles an hour, ankle-high, from the edge of the bat to the fielder standing a few yards away in the slips. A second later that fieldsman finds himself (assuming he is better than I am) lying full stretch on the ground, with the ball clutched in his hand. He has made no conscious decision to get there. He has, through pre-programming (practice, we call it), calculated velocities, distances and angles, and instructed his muscles accordingly. The robot does the same on a much more primitive level.

But what about the fielder faced with a choice? The oppositions need only four runs to win. If he goes for the catch but misses, then the other side wins; if he concentrates just on stopping the ball, the issue stays open. There – still sub-consciously – the fielder makes an instant qualitative decision. Put that into machine terms and you have a consciousness problem – unless, as in the chess analogy, you can conceive of programming for any eventuality. Gregory agrees there is a difference there – 'the difference of the machine clearly going beyond its programming or the theory of its circuitry'.

But that line of argument does not worry the quantitative school. Their answer is the Turing Test. Alan Turing, a British mathematician whose contribution to the emergence of the computer was mentioned in Chapter 4, devised this test: put a person in a room where there are two computer terminals, one connected to a computer, the other managed by another human being. If the tester, in his conversations via the keyboard, cannot distinguish which is which, then you have the thinking machine. Many people – including computer scientists – have been deceived in this way for quite a while, but no machine has yet passed a rigorous Turing Test.

In any event, we don't have to reach the borders of the Turing Test – let alone get involved with questions about whether machines can grow emotions – before we come up against the truly intelligent machine which makes its own decisions. There are programming techniques being developed which will enable the computer to re-program itself to meet changed circumstances. In a limited sense that happens already.

The optimists ally these developments with the vast stores of information that can be put at a computer's disposal, and the speed at which the computer can use that information, to foresee the inevitable emergence of the ultra-intelligent machine which, as our logical superior, will help human society out of its illogical difficulties.

The pessimists see such machines both as a tool for tidy totalitarianism and as a threat in themselves. As Frank George, professor of cybernetics at Brunel University, London, has put it, how will we be able to pull the plug out of such a computer when it can control its environment through, say, the robots it runs?

This is where the theories of artificial intelligence and the physical realities of the next generation of computers meet. John Barker, a quantum physicist who commutes between Warwick University in the English Midlands and Colorado State University at the foot of the Rockies (where he is affiliate professor of theoretical physics), believes that the sub-micron microelectronics now being tested in the laboratories will behave in some ways like biological cells.

A micron is one thousandth part of a millimetre, and lines thinner than that have already been put experimentally on silicon. Barker says that once you get below half a micron, you cannot scale down once again. It calls for a completely new way of looking at things. Systems this small are 'essentially synergistic and have powers of self-organization'; if one part ceases to function, the rest of the system may take over the work of its own accord.

Also, says Barker, synergistic systems get us beyond having to think in terms of sequential computing, in which calculations are made in single sequences. Until the late 1970s all conventional computers worked that way, but there are now faster computers that come a bit closer to human ways of operation by using an army of silicon chips operating in parallel.

Such computers have achieved speeds of around 100 million calculations a second. One of the first to demonstrate that speed was ICL's Distributed Array Processor, which uses 20,480 chips working in parallel. The speed comes not only from parallel working but also from the fact that the chips are physically close together, so that (just as in the chips themselves) the messages don't have far to travel. The individual chips operate about ten times faster than those that run the routine pocket calculator. The prototype Distributed Array Processor was about the size of a wardrobe and also needed an outside computer to organize its work. Later versions, using higher-powered chips, should fit in a suitcase.

But the post-chip computer could make even that look trivial. There is the possibility by 1984, or thereabouts, of prototype computers working close to the speed of light in temperatures near absolute zero. We have already seen that the silicon chip has brought to reality what used to be just computer-science theory – the theory that the computer can perform any task that its human instructors can precisely define. We have also seen that current technology holds the theoretical possibility of producing computers smarter than ourselves. So why go further?

There are reasons more practically compelling than insatiable curiosity. Economic forces are already pressing for computers that will work at faster speeds than the silicon chip can manage. Even if (as indicated back in Chapter 4) the semi-conductor industry itself becomes less boisterous, the computer industry has ample motivation to search far ahead. The immediate demand for faster computers comes from the military and the scientists. Computers tracking missiles, computers in weather forecasting or in astronomy, in aircraft design or the modelling of national economies, all need to juggle with massive mathematical problems in three dimensions and at higher speeds than current computers can offer; and that demand is beginning to spread into the commercial world with the advance of computer networks carrying hundreds of remote terminals.

The United States' defence budget for 1980 included the first 30 million dollars of a 200-million dollar, six-year programme to produce much faster integrated circuits, and teams involving thirty companies have applied to the Department of Defense for a share of that programme. Another example of the trend is the decision of the National Aeronautical and Space Administration to order for use by around 1985 a computer forty times more powerful than anything in operation today. That machine will be employed on the horrendous equations needed in the design of aircraft. It will save aero engineers the expensive and time-consuming series of tests in wind tunnels and should also produce aircraft designs more precisely directed at saving fuel.

The physicists can now glimpse the end of the road for orthodox silicon. Therefore, long-dormant candidates to succeed the silicon chip are getting renewed attention in the laboratories. But there is still a long road to that final wall. Dr Robert Dennard, of IBM's research centre at Yorktown Heights, New York, puts the practical limit at chip lines a quarter of a micron wide – that is one hundred thousandth of an inch, twenty times tighter than the lines on today's front-line chips. Below that level the problems become too intense. If you view a chip line five microns wide under an electron microscope, it looks like a mountain range, with wobbly foothills and jagged peaks. It doesn't vitally matter at that size. But reduce the size by a factor of ten, without equivalent increases in precision, and you are lost. In production, the electron beams bombarding the chip to make those lines start to bounce like tennis balls, spreading their largesse beyond the target area. In design, a problem already being encountered is that the speed of the message along the lines does not increase to match the overall speed of the total device.

IBM's best practical result so far announced is an experimental chip four millimetres by four millimetres. That holds 256,000 bits of information and operates at a speed of a billionth of a second. But a better bet in storage terms may be the bubble memory (as we saw in Chapter 4). The laboratory score in this technology is four million bits (say sixteen pages of a phone directory) on a one-square-centimetre chip.

The search for speed beyond the capabilities of silicon centres (in work that has been made public anyway) on two possibilities that have been around for more than a decade – Josephson Junctions and the 111-V compounds.

The materials called 111-V compounds – such as gallium arsenide and gallium phosphide – allow electrons to work more zippily than they can in silicon. The 111-V compounds are already used in opto-electronics. Their use in computers interests the military, particularly in the United States. One drawback is that the materials cost about £100 a square centimetre, though there is now the possibility of producing layers of gallium arsenide four inches across, which should bring the price down. A 1980 report of Infotech International estimated that gallium arsenide chips will be freely available by the mid-1980s, and will be working six times faster than silicon.

The theory of the Josephson Junction came from a Cambridge physicist, Brian Josephson, who won the Nobel Prize in 1962 for predicting the effect. At temperatures near absolute zero (minus 273 degrees Centigrade, the temperature at which molecular movement ceases) certain metals lose their resistance to current – they become superconductors. The Josephson Junction uses this fact to provide a switch that will operate close to the speed of light in the materials used. Magnetic fields (and direct injections of current) are used to suppress the superconductivity and provide the 'off' state of the switch. A Josephson Junction handles the nought-or-one bits of computer information in that fashion.

The junctions are being used in many national standards laboratories. measuring voltage very precisely. IBM has been experimenting with them for computers since 1971, suspending the circuits in liquid helium to provide a temperature of minus 269. But Peter Wolf, who heads the work at IBM's laboratory in Zurich, is cautious about progress. He says it is hard to predict when Josephson computers will be in use. The next step is to produce a small prototype computer, 'by 1984 or so'. Wolf explains the silicon chip's limitations in this way: 'Assume you want to build a computer to carry out 250 million calculations a second. You could not allow any line to be longer than 7·5 centimetres, and you would need to pack a billion parts in a shoebox-sized cube. Silicon chips would not be fast enough. They would consume too much power, produce too much heat, they would melt. A similar cube of Josephson Junctions should do the work with ten watts of power.'

IBM's Josephson Junctions have so far operated at thirteen trillionths of a second. The actual switching time has been cut to seven trillionths, but another six trillionths are needed for the message to travel from one circuit to the next. That corresponds to the speed of light in the circuits used. Even so, Wolf says, sober-faced: 'The speed of light is not good enough for our requirements.'

Josephson still brings us back to silicon in a way. The likely basis for Josephson computers would be a foundation of silicon, though the circuits themselves rely on a microscopic sandwich of metal alloys and insulators.

Beyond Josephson, we get hazier. Barron and Curnow plumped for one of the possibilities in their report on microelectronics to the UK Department of Industry. They suggested devices created by exploiting the wave characteristics of electrons rather than their bulk characteristics, like current or voltage.

Another area attracting research is the optical representation of information. Four scientists at another IBM laboratory – San Jose in California – have patented a laser method of recording data which should be able to put the capacity of the human brain on a surface measuring a yard by a yard (that is, if you accept the estimate that, in computer terms, the human memory can hold only ten million million bits).

The authors of US Patent No. 4,101,976 are George Castro, manager of the physical science department at San Jose, and his colleagues Dietrich Haarer, Roger Macfarlane and Peter Trommsdorff. They emphasize that they have a long way to go before their idea becomes everyday practicality, but they seem confident of producing an array of tiny recording blocks – 100 million of them packed into a square centimetre and each one of those 100 million holding 1000 bits of information.

These blocks contain photoreactive material; and a tuneable dye laser is used to 'burn holes' in them. The laser beam selects the particular block to be used, either to record information or to extract it. But – and here comes the quantum jump – by varying the frequency of the laser light it is possible to 'talk to' many different groups of molecules within each block. Each setting of the laser frequency produces a chemical reaction in the material, transforming a small percentage of its photoreactive molecules into a different compound. The loss of the original molecules causes a gap – the burnt hole.

So: presence or absence of holes equals nought-or-one bits. But in this case the message is there not only in three-dimensional space but also in a sort of fourth dimension – by its frequency location in terms of the tuning of the laser. Thus thousands of bits could be stored in one speck of material only one twenty-five-thousandth of an inch across.

Castro is experimenting with several storage materials. A more primitive cousin of that style of recording computer information was ready for use at the start of the 1980s. This is the use of laser-read discs of the kind used in video recording. Such discs provide high-quality sound and pictures, even if the disc is roughly handled or left uncleaned, because the laser light seeks out the message through dirt or distortions. Castro says: 'Hole-burning breathes new life into optical storage by theoretically extending that density a few orders of magnitude.'

But the Castro idea, too, requires temperatures near absolute zero. In the experiments so far the photoreactive molecules have been suspended in tubes of frozen organic liquids or polymers.

If the thought of such deep-freeze computers disturbs our primeval pre-programmed prejudices, then we can turn for comfort to Edward de Bono, the psychologist who fathered the concept of lateral thinking. He has produced his own definition of the self-aware computer: it will have a sense of humour. The computer that thinks – and he believes it is 'not so far away' – will look at the world in different ways from those its programmers intended. It will blend into the pattern-making universe which is now emerging and will be ready to switch patterns when triggered by the incongruous – the sense of humour.

De Bono is disappointed that computer people are still not very conceptual and he has held a series of tutorials to try to re-educate them. He says they tend to be essentially librarians, classifying and processing information. The second computing generation will take the pattern-making road, just as philosophy has moved on from the Germanic classification approach. The danger is, he says, that this second generation may not emerge with sufficient speed to match the expansion of computing across society. He believes that the model-making capabilities of the coming computers – and, remember, they already enable businesses and governments to make forecasts which they could never statistically manage before – will have an even greater impact on society than automation.

De Bono envisages three ages of the self-aware computer. First, the personal servant; the computer which will relate to the individual's needs, providing solutions to problems one stage further – and quicker – than the individual could himself, while eliminating the emotional factors in human reasoning, like getting out of bed on the wrong side. Then the group intelligence – the computer that will solve problems from the input of a corporate group of people, And, finally – 'much more difficult to achieve' – the solution to problems on a societal scale.

But is all that lateral enough? When Alvin Toffler wrote *Future Shock* the microprocessor was just leaving the drawing board, ready to upset the timescale. Now bio-engineering is sharp on the horizon.

I received a timely lesson on the immutability of change on the day in the mid-1970s when I saw my first microprocessor. It was at a trade exhibition which seemed more like Tiffany's. The chips glittered on plush trays like intricate pieces of jewellery. When I sighted their inner reality through the microscope it was like the aerial view of Manhattan on a clear day. Never was I more in danger of being gadget-happy.

Luckily, the exhibition was being opened by Professor Eric Laithwaite of Imperial College, London, an engineer who tears up orthodoxies with the relish of Richmal Crompton's William. The line he took was not a Friends of the Earth one, nor even the then newly fashionable power-from-the-plants approach. It went like this: we have certainly got it wrong in terms of root efficiency. Human ingenuity is not yet one-per-cent employed. We have let our machines evolve instead of redesigning them. The result is a stagnation that is only now being upset after half a century. And the upsetter – microelectronics – is in danger of thinking that it has nearly reached such a plateau itself. What microelectronics can do on a sliver of silicon, nature does on a speck of dust. Nature rejects the wheel, nature rejects metal. We have to think of something more organic, perhaps even alive, to make the next tremendous leap. When naturally produced fluid magnetic circuits are set free to take the shapes they like, they are not the shapes of man-made mathematics; they are the shapes of ferns and leaves and forked lightning. We should grow our technology like plants ... Today, bio-electronics, bio-engineering, bio-physics, bio-chemistry are beginning to do just that.

17. The naked emperor

Thirteen of the sixteen chapters that have gone before have dealt with the facts of the present day, not with guesses about the future. Now I would like to draw just one personal conclusion – or rather a dawning suspicion – from those facts.

Back in 1976, Alex Reid, the head of Prestel, who was then one of the British Post Office's strategic planners, presented a prescient paper about the challenges that have since become more clearly understood. He was not alone, of course, but it was mainly such computer specialists, plus a few newspapers and magazines, who were then becoming agitated about society's failure to prepare ground rules for the changes in lifestyle that a post-industrial society could bring. Reid said that the social effects of expanding information systems presented 'opportunities and dangers of profound concern to all'. At the organizational level, he forecast paradoxical development: 'In one sense telecommunications will facilitate the growth of multinational corporations. But in another sense they will allow small and specialized organizations to flourish.' This duality would persist at national level, dispersing office work from the cities to rural centres; and the duality would be at its most acute at the global level – 'In the long term we must surely accept ... increased inter-dependence tending towards McLuhan's global village.'

The choice then facing us would be 'a joyous celebration of evolutionary climax' or inefficiency, dehumanization and totalitarianism. And Reid placed the central responsibility for guiding that choice on the media:

It is in facing fundamental and long-term questions that the political mechanism (with its understandable electoral preoccupations) seems weakest. Although these questions are political, it is perhaps asking too much to expect politicians to provide the intellectual leadership in their analysis. This brings us to the crucial role of journalists, authors, and academics in raising and analysing questions concerning the social impact of telecommunications. Unless these questions are common currency, and widely understood, unless there is a lively generation of strategies for their solution, unless all this is underpinned with a sound theoretical understanding of the processes at work, there is little hope of our responding wisely to these challenging opportunities and dangers.

At that time the sentence that caught in my craw was the one about not expecting too much from politicians. In my apolitical naivety I thought he could not be right. Surely, by 1980 at least, politicians would have realized that they had to lift their heads from their four-year timetables and consult their mass masters about the real changes that were gathering speed below the surface.

But from far left to far right in British politics proper, as well as in trade unions, industrial managements and the civil service hierarchies, the overwhelming message has been: 'You'll have to change but, of course, we in The System won't.' Only a handful of influential people (of random political persuasion) have dared to suggest that it might be a good idea to look at the Protestant work ethic and see whether we actually believe in it.

There the suspicion arises, a suspicion directed equally at the 'Right to Work' campaigners and the presidents of multinational corporations. A world in which we no longer worked to live, and only lived to work if we wanted to, might destroy every power base and potential power base. Who would be a politician in an actual democracy where every decision could be taken by the public in a push-button home vote? What managing director would thrive on his twelve-hour day running an enterprise creating huge wealth but with only a dozen highly independent specialists to manage? And what point trade unions?

There is the fundamental challenge of the chip and its brighter successors – challenging our assumptions about initiativeless employment in big clusters, threatening the people-managing delights of business, unions and politics, and pointing to the economic viability of living in smaller, less pressurized communities. Of course, all that would be decades away in any event – and it is blinkered from all the other aspects of human insanity, like nuclear stockpiles. But the 1970s have at least shown the economic practicality of what has been there in theory since the computer was born.

In immediate terms, the chip has exposed an equally lethal truth. If it is now actually becoming cheaper to let the machine take over many lifeless jobs – tending production lines in noisy, energy-wasting factories; typing other people's letters and travelling in sardine-tin trains for the privilege; risking life underground or underwater – why are millions of people still spending most of their waking hours doing them? If that's a naive question, it's the naivety of seeing the emperor naked.

Suggestions for further reading

General

Iann Barron and Ray Curnow, *The Future of Microelectronics*: Frances Pinter, 1979.

Christopher Evans, *The Mighty Micro*: Victor Gollancz, 1979.

Roger Hunt and John Shelley, *Computers and Commonsense*: Prentice Hall International, 1975.

The semi-conductor industry

Ernest Braun and Stuart MacDonald, *Revolution in Miniature*: Cambridge University Press, 1978.

Artificial intelligence

Margaret Boden, *Artificial Intelligence and Natural Man*: Harvester Press, 1977.

Frank George, *Machine Takeover*: Pergamon, 1977.

Joseph Weizenbaum, *Computer Power and Human Reason*: W. H. Freeman and Co., 1977.

Telecommunications

James Martin, *The Wired Society*: Prentice Hall, 1978.

Employment

Clive Jenkins and Barrie Sherman, *The Collapse of Work*: Eyre Methuen, 1979.

The Micro Revolution

Roy Rothwell and Walter Zegveld, *Technical Change and Employment*: Frances Pinter, 1979.

Crime

Thomas Whiteside, *Computer Capers*: Sidgwick and Jackson, 1979.

Kenneth Wong, *Risk Analysis and Control*: NCC Publications and Hayden Book Company, 1977.

Privacy

Patricia Hewitt (ed.), *Computer, Records and the Right to Privacy*: Input Two-Nine, 1979.

Report of the Committee on Data Protection: HMSO Command 7341, 1978.

Viewdata

Sam Fedida and Rex Malik, *The Viewdata Revolution*: Associated Business Press, 1979.

Rex Winsbury, *Electronic Bookstall*: International Institute of Communications, 1979.

Index

213

Index

Fontana Paperbacks

Fontana is a leading paperback publisher of fiction and non-fiction, with authors ranging from Alistair MacLean, Agatha Christie and Desmond Bagley to Solzhenitsyn and Pasternak, from Gerald Durrell and Joy Adamson to the famous Modern Masters series.

In addition to a wide-ranging collection of internationally popular writers of fiction, Fontana also has an outstanding reputation for history, natural history, military history, psychology, psychiatry, politics, economics, religion and the social sciences.

All Fontana books are available at your bookshop or newsagent; or can be ordered direct. Just fill in the form and list the titles you want.

FONTANA BOOKS, Cash Sales Department, G.P.O. Box 29, Douglas, Isle of Man, British Isles. Please send purchase price, plus 8p per book. Customers outside the U.K. send purchase price, plus 10p per book. Cheque, postal or money order. No currency.

NAME (Block letters)

ADDRESS